3 WINS!

Turn Talent Uncertainty into Predictable Growth...

and Scalable REVENUE

Kent Wessinger, PhD

First Paperback Edition

Published by Freiling Agency, LLC.

P.O. Box 1264

Warrenton, VA 20188 www.FreilingAgency.com

PB ISBN: 978-1-969826-12-2

E-book ISBN: 978-1-969826-13-9

I dedicate this book to my 3 GREATEST WINS...

my children Carson, Maggie and Sam.

"Show me Your ways,
Teach me Your paths,
Guide me in Your truth."

— Psalms 25:3–4

The 3 WINS Framework

The **3** WINS framework operates on three inevitable outcomes:

WIN #1 (ATTRACT): When clarity makes growth visible, talent comes to you—predictably.

WIN #2 (ENGAGE): When accountability builds trust, engagement follows.

WIN #3 (RETAIN): When community secures the future, people stay—and revenue follows.

These are not principles.

They are tested outcomes, produced by design.

TABLE OF CONTENTS

CHAPTER 1

The Talent Crisis Is a Revenue Crisis

IN PRIVATE BOARDROOMS ACROSS THE COUNTRY, one question continues to surface with increasing frequency:

Can I trust the younger workforce with the future of this company?

It is rarely voiced publicly—but it shapes executive behavior daily.

In 2020, **48%** of seasoned leaders admitted concern about the future of their organizations with younger employees. Today, that number has surged to **83%**. This is not a temporary anxiety. It reflects a measurable shift in leadership confidence.

Concern does not stay abstract. It shows up in softened expectations, hesitant accountability, diluted standards, and performance reviews designed to avoid conflict rather than reinforce growth. Over time, that hesitation reshapes culture. Accountability weakens. Trust erodes. Alignment fractures.

And when alignment fractures, growth slows.

> *Organizations rarely collapse because of flawed strategy. They deteriorate when leaders lose confidence in the people responsible for executing it.*

THE SILENT WAR FOR TALENT

The dominant executive question has evolved.

It used to be: "What's wrong with Millennials?"

Now it's more direct—and more dangerous: "Are younger generations a threat to the future of my company?"

That question is not just skepticism. It is a signal of uncertainty as familiar leadership frameworks stop producing results.

The problem is that most solutions offered—consultants, books, trend reports—are built on weak data: small sample sizes, personal opinion, and sweeping generalizations that amplify fear instead of solving it.

Across **54,000** participants in thirty-four countries, **64%** of leaders indicated they view the younger workforce as a threat to stability.

When leaders see their future talent pool as a liability, defensive behavior follows.

They build policies instead of pathways.

They emphasize control over clarity.

They manage behavior instead of developing capability.

The result is not stronger performance. It is friction.

At the same time, when Millennials and Gen Z describe themselves, the most consistent responses are: creative, collaborative, and capable.

The gap between perception and self-perception is not philosophical—it is operational.

> *When leaders interpret intensity as entitlement and ambition as fragility, distrust becomes structural.*

And structural distrust carries financial consequences.

Replacing a high-performing employee often costs at least their annual salary once lost productivity, rehiring, and retraining are accounted for. Multiply that across preventable attrition, and what appears to be a cultural issue becomes a margin issue.

THE REVENUE CONSEQUENCE

Even the strongest product cannot compensate for disengaged execution.

When a workforce lacks clarity around expectations, growth, and advancement:

- performance variability increases
- retention declines
- revenue is affected

21%

of organizations report having a defined strategy to attract, engage, and retain talent. Only **16%** have one that consistently works for Millennials and Gen Z.

> *This is not evidence of generational weakness. It is evidence of architecture failure.*

The younger workforce does not follow brands. It follows visible opportunity.

When organizations fail to construct a clearly defined path of growth and success, high-potential employees redirect their effort elsewhere.

In competitive markets, the absence of clarity becomes a recruitment advantage—for someone else.

THE STRUCTURAL BLIND SPOT

Many leaders attribute disengagement to motivation. Others cite entitlement or generational fragility.

These interpretations misdiagnose the issue.

The problem is structural.

Previous generations navigated careers with directional guidance: work hard, stay loyal, and progress would follow. That worked in stable environments.

Today's workforce operates in volatility—digital acceleration, fluid career mobility, and constant disruption.

Direction is no longer enough.

Ambiguity does not signal freedom. It signals risk.

> *You offered a compass. They are asking for a map.*

A map provides milestones, defined competencies, measurable progression, and visible opportunity. Without it, employees drift—then disengage—or leave.

WHAT THE DATA REVEALED

This book is built on thirty-five structured questions comparing how generations think, work, and define leadership. What began as a **500**-person sample expanded into one of the most comprehensive generational workforce datasets available—over **54,000** participants across thirty-four nations.

> *Data alone does not change companies. Implementation does.*

Across startups, Fortune 100 companies, healthcare systems, engineering firms, telecom organizations, government agencies, financial institutions, print industry, the pattern repeated:

Where structure was installed, outcomes stabilized. Where structure was absent, performance remained unpredictable.

The conclusion was not theoretical. It was architectural.

> *Most leadership books attempt to inspire better behavior. This system engineers it.*

Sustainable performance requires a system that produces three outcomes:

- attracting capable talent
- engaging them through structured accountability
- retaining them through meaningful progression

When those outcomes are designed intentionally, revenue follows—not by chance, but by structure.

FROM CONCERN TO STRUCTURE

Leaders are not suffering from a lack of information. They are overwhelmed by it.

Trends, opinions, and reactive commentary create activity—but rarely produce structure.

Concerned leadership is reactive. It softens expectations to prevent attrition and substitutes caution for clarity.

Confident leadership is structural.

It defines expectations precisely. It reinforces accountability consistently. It aligns development with measurable outcomes.

Confidence is not optimism. It is disciplined clarity applied over time.

The central question is not whether the younger workforce is capable of carrying the future.

The evidence is clear—it is.

The real question is whether leadership systems are designed to channel that capability effectively.

INSTALLING THE ARCHITECTURE

This book introduces the **3** WINS Operating System™—a unified leadership framework built on three interdependent strands:

Clarity. Accountability. Community.

Clarity attracts capable people because it removes ambiguity. Accountability engages them because it reinforces growth. Community retains them because it converts participation into commitment.

When these strands operate together, talent volatility stabilizes—and revenue becomes predictable.

The younger workforce—the largest segment of the labor market—is not waiting for organizations to adapt. They are building their future within or beyond your company.

The variable is not generational disposition. It is leadership design.

Final Charge

The younger workforce is not the risk—it is the greatest underleveraged asset in the modern economy.

When given clarity, reinforced through accountability, and developed within a system that builds real community, this generation does not resist performance—it accelerates it.

The organizations that recognize this shift will not simply stabilize their workforce; they will outpace their competitors.

What follows is not a theory of better leadership.

It is the architecture required to build it— one that transforms uncertainty into alignment, alignment into performance, and performance into predictable growth.

CHAPTER 2

Concern Kills. Confidence WINS.

CONCERN IS NOT A MINDSET. It's a measurable leadership condition—and it's expensive.

A DEFINING MOMENT IN THE DATA

In January 2020, I made a pivotal decision in my ongoing research: I drew a line in the data to track how the post-pandemic era was reshaping leadership and workforce dynamics.

Since then, the results have been both revealing and alarming. While some behaviors have returned to pre-COVID norms, others have shifted dramatically—especially one escalating trend that cannot be ignored:

The soaring level of concern from seasoned leaders regarding the future of their company with younger employees.

When seasoned leaders are asked a simple question:

"Are you concerned about the future of your organization with the younger workforce?"

Their responses illuminate a troubling reality that's ensnaring even the most experienced executives.

In 2020, **48%** of leaders said yes—they were concerned about their organization's future with younger employees. Today, that number has rocketed to **83%**.

> *That's not just an increase—it's a crisis.*

Concern isn't just an emotion; it's a line item—showing up in turnover, stalled initiatives, and lost revenue.

And the outcome of an organization led by a concerned leader is as predictable as it is costly:

Concern breeds uncertainty into the culture.

It clouds decision-making, thwarts innovation, and leaves growth to chance. When bold action is needed most, concern paralyzes momentum and drives friction.

This paralysis is exactly why the **3** WINS Operating System matters now—to move leaders from concern to clarity, from reaction to strategy.

So let me ask:

Are you concerned about the future of your company with the younger workforce?

And more importantly—

What happens if you do nothing?

PERSPECTIVE

A few years ago, my youngest son, Sam, called with unexpected news:

> "*Hey Dad, guess what I did today? I joined the Army National Guard.*"

Before I could fully process what he'd just said, he was already off to Fort Sill, Oklahoma, for Basic Training. Fourteen weeks later, I sat in 117-degree heat, surrounded by thousands of proud families, waiting for the graduation ceremony to begin.

As two companies of soldiers marched onto the field with flawless precision, a one-star general took the mic and declared:

"Ladies and gentlemen! What stands before you is the greatest military in the history of the world!"

The greatest in the history of the world?

At first, I was surprised by the confidence of that claim. But as I scanned the field, something shifted.

My surprise turned into conviction.

Every soldier standing before us—every single one—was a Millennial or Gen Z.

And that general, backed by decades of experience, intelligence, and leadership, wasn't guessing. He was declaring a truth he had seen firsthand.

So, I asked myself:

If one of the most respected institutions on the planet defines this generation as the greatest in history—

Why are eight out of ten business leaders still concerned?

What are we missing? And more importantly—

What potential are we failing to unlock?

DIGGING DOWN: CONCERNED VS. CONFIDENT LEADERSHIP

Concern isn't neutral—it shapes behavior.

Concerned leaders create cultures marked by:

- Hesitation
- Uncertainty
- Fear-based decision-making
- Random, reactive strategies

That kind of leadership feeds conflict—especially generational conflict. It leaves growth to chance.

Confident leadership does the opposite. It builds cultures driven by:

- Strategic clarity
- Structured growth
- Organizational alignment
- A shared sense of purpose

And at the heart of confidence? Active accountability.

In high-performing cultures, accountability isn't avoided—it's expected. It's not feared—it's trusted. It's woven into the daily rhythm of leadership at every level.

THE POWER OF ACCOUNTABILITY

Here's what the data makes clear:

83%

of leaders are operating from concern. Only **17%** are actively building cultures of confidence.

Accountability draws the line between mediocrity and momentum. Where accountability is actively present, culture strengthens, strategy thrives, people rise, and growth follows.

So, ask yourself:

Are you leading with concern—or with confidence?

Are you reacting to your workforce—or preparing them to lead?

Are you uncertain about what's next—or charting it with clarity?

If you're stuck in the middle, this chapter is your call to shift—now.

THE REALITY LEADERS ARE FACING

When leaders reach out to me for guidance, the conversation often begins with a tone of frustration.

They're overwhelmed, burned out, and unsure how to connect with the younger workforce. I consistently hear these five concerns:

> *"They want a six-figure salary after six months of work."*
>
> *"They don't even show up for interviews."*
>
> *"There's generational tension inside my building that I can't seem to resolve."*
>
> *"They want emotional safety but avoid accountability."*
>
> *"I'm afraid if I hold them accountable, they'll quit."*

These aren't complaints from bitter, outdated leaders looking for someone to blame. None of these frustrations are fabricated. Each one reflects real, repeatable patterns—observable behaviors that are breeding high levels of concern among seasoned executives.

And while each of these issues can be destructive, they are also valid and solvable. They are not signs of a broken generation; they're signals pointing toward the path of sustainable growth.

These patterns all point to one underlying issue that determines whether culture thrives or collapses:

> *Accountability.*

That's why the **3** WINS is built to address each root issue—helping leaders WIN Talent, WIN Engagement, and WIN Retention through clarity, accountability and community.

Lead What's Next — Final Charge: Concern Kills. Confidence WINS.

That's how confident leaders build strong cultures—and stronger people.

You've seen the numbers. You've felt the tension. You know in your gut that leading from concern is not sustainable. Concern may feel responsible—it may even feel safe—but it quietly sabotages your people and your culture.

Confidence isn't arrogance. It isn't ignoring challenges or sugarcoating reality. Confidence is clarity in motion.

Concern clouds leadership. Clarity restores it.

And that is where we turn next.

The younger workforce is not waiting for leaders to feel ready. They are building their future within or beyond your organization. The variable is not generational disposition. It is leadership design.

The next chapter begins with the most important leadership discipline in the modern workforce: clarity. Because when clarity is established, growth becomes visible—and momentum can begin.

CHAPTER 3

Clarity: Remove the Barriers. Reveal the Path.

LEAD WITH CLARITY

YOU'RE NOT LOSING THE YOUNGER WORKFORCE because you can't compete with perks—you're losing them because clarity has been missing from the conversation.

While leaders sprint to roll out remote Fridays, safe spaces, and wellness stipends, younger employees are quietly asking a far more transformational question:

"What's my path to growth and success here?"

Perks fade. Pay scales flatten. But clarity creates commitment, ignites momentum, and turns potential into performance.

Clarity is THE new leadership currency—an asset that fortifies your growth across every generation.

A clear vision must be operationalized into daily experience—or people drift.

They want to know:

- What am I building toward?
- Who's going to help me get there?
- What's the timeline, and how is progress measured?

If these questions go unanswered, someone else will answer them—and they'll win the talent you can't afford to lose. And that 'someone else' might be your competitor—or TikTok, where they build their own brand instead of yours.

When employees can see the path—when they know what's expected, how to succeed, and how to grow—they stay, contribute, and thrive.

The challenge for every leader is this: the more you invest in clarity, the greater your return in performance, loyalty, and leadership.

> *Clarity doesn't cost—it compounds.*

My research and implementation experience show this: organizations that provide a clearly defined path to growth don't just grow—they win the talent war and scale revenue.

Before you can build a clearly defined path of growth and success, you must first identify and remove the structural barriers quietly holding your organization back.

In this chapter, we confront three barriers standing between you and the **3** WINS: generational conflict, diluted accountability, and a distorted view of the younger workforce.

Before we confront those barriers, you need one lens: when vision stays trapped in leadership language instead of operationalized into daily experience, people don't resist—they drift.

To prevent drift, we must first define the system that stops it. I refer to this framework as the **3** WINS Operating System. It is built on three interdependent strands—Clarity, Accountability, and Community—that must function together to sustain belief, momentum, and commitment over time. When one strand weakens, engagement erodes. When all three are intentionally designed and reinforced, growth becomes predictable.

WHEN VISION FAILS, PEOPLE WANDER

"Where there is no vision, the people wander." – Proverbs 29:18

Vision isn't ambition. It's revealed direction—a trustworthy path forward. When that direction is missing, people drift. Drift looks like disengagement, quiet job searches, and turnover leaders blame on "the market."

That's the leadership blind spot: executives may have vision, but vision locked in the C-suite doesn't restrain behavior on the front lines. Vision must be experienced, not announced.

This is where most leadership teams get it wrong. They try to communicate their way out of a structural problem.

CLARITY IS NOT COMMUNICATION — IT IS ARCHITECTURE

This is where the **3** WINS Operating System makes growth, engagement, and retention predictable. Ecclesiastes calls it a cord that "is not quickly broken"—not poetry, engineering.

Install the system, not the idea.

This is not a model to understand. This is a system to install.

The **3** WINS Operating System makes Engagement and Retention predictable when three strands operate together:

- Clarity – a visible growth path people can trust
- Accountability – relationships fortified in trust and follow-through
- Community – belonging that turns work into commitment... and revenue

The three strands in the **3** WINS Operating System do not sit beside the **3** WINS—they power them.

> *Clarity attracts. Accountability engages. Community retains.*

—and when the barriers below are addressed with precision, they unlock three high-impact outcomes:

- ELIMINATE generational conflict that drains energy, trust, and momentum
- OPEN the gate to accountability gate for sustainable growth
- CLARIFY the truth about the "threat" younger generations pose

WHO IS YOUR TOBIAH?

Every collapse begins the same way: leadership defenses fail long before the future does.

When Nehemiah was commissioned to fortify the future of Jerusalem, his first move wasn't construction—it was excavation.

The city was exposed. Vulnerable. The wall that once protected its people had collapsed—leaving behind a mountain of rubble that buried the foundation.

Nehemiah understood a timeless truth: you cannot fortify the future on buried weakness.

He knew the future couldn't rise on a buried foundation. The debris had to go—not because it didn't matter in the past, but because it had no place in the future.

But the greatest resistance to fortifying the city didn't come from outside forces. It came from inside—from a respected, long-tenured leader named Tobiah.

He had grown content with the vulnerability and fought the fortification. Why?

First, Nehemiah was a new, young face—bringing fresh ideas, new perspectives, and an uncommon passion for the city. He never pretended to have all the answers. He was simply burdened by what was broken—the collapsed wall, the vulnerability of the people—and compelled to help rebuild. He wasn't seeking control; he was offering contribution. Yet that very willingness was interpreted as a threat.

Second, because the rubble of the wall had become familiar. It had woven itself into the rhythm of daily life. They had adapted to antiquated perspectives—and defined it as normal.

This wasn't just about broken bricks—it was about broken mindsets. The debris had become sacred, blinding him to the urgent need for fortification. Worst of all, Tobiah quietly pulled others into his cave of resistance, convincing them to defend the very rubble that threatened their future.

That's why the first barrier is always internal: somewhere in your organization, there's a Tobiah protecting the rubble of "how we've always done it" from the clarity your future requires.

And as long as Tobiah goes unchallenged, comfort will always outrun clarity, derailing growth and suppressing revenue.

So, here's your leadership audit:

- What internal voices are resisting progress under the disguise of "stability"?
- Which policies, systems, or beliefs are no longer strategic—but still sacred?
- Who's your Tobiah? Who's protecting outdated practices in the name of tradition?

CLARITY: THE REAL SAFE SPACE

While many seasoned leaders instinctively roll their eyes at the idea of "safe spaces" – and I was once firmly in that camp – the real issue isn't the designated safe-space room, the rooftop, or even the aesthetics. It's about what we believe those spaces represent. We misjudge them as signs of entitlement or softness, labeling younger workers as fragile snowflakes, when in reality we've misunderstood the request entirely.

> *They're not asking for escape.*
> *They're asking for clarity.*

A safe space isn't about avoiding work; it's about clearing the fog that blocks meaningful work. It's where confusion lifts, direction returns, and purpose regains its footing.

The structural failure is clear:

Clarity doesn't coddle; it equips. That's why it's the ultimate safe space.

Give people clarity, and they won't need a room to retreat to — they'll have the confidence to advance.

The answer was never a room. The answer is clarity.

RESPECT IS FIDUCIARY

I often hear seasoned leaders say, "These younger generations don't respect us. They don't understand the sacrifice it took to build this company."

But here's a reality check: Respect isn't sentimental. Respect is fiduciary.

You don't earn respect from the younger workforce by reminding them of what you endured — you earn it by investing in what they need to succeed. And if, after that investment, they still refuse to reciprocate, let them walk.

The ultimate form of respect is clarity.

Respect your talent enough to give them direction.

Respect them enough to hold them accountable.

Respect them enough to place them in meaningful, intense, growth-focused roles.

But most importantly: Respect them with clarity – clarity about expectations, clarity about outcomes, clarity about the path ahead.

Younger generations aren't disrespectful; they're responding to the absence of what every high-performing person requires: a clear, structured environment where they can WIN.

Respect isn't about age, hierarchy, or longevity.

Respect is a leader's willingness to provide clarity that matches the employee's desire to contribute.

COMFORT: THE HIDDEN ENEMY OF CLARITY

The phrase "this is how we've always done it" is the corporate version of a "safe space."

Ironically, the same senior employees who mock "safe spaces" often cling the tightest to the comfort of outdated models—because the status quo feels safer than change.

I've seen this pattern play out in every sector—from family-run businesses to Fortune 500 giants.

Sometimes, a direct, growth-focused conversation with those employees flips the switch—they see the bigger picture and get on board.

Other times, they double down, dig in, and escalate their resistance. That's when well-meaning leaders bring me in to speak directly to their Tobiahs—the long-tenured employees whose loyalty to the past outweighs their fear of the future.

Some shift. Some stay. Others leave.

But make no mistake—inaction is a decision. I've witnessed generational conflict dismantle companies built to thrive.

And choosing comfort over clarity will cost you far more than one employee. It will cost you momentum. Innovation. Top-tier talent.

They're afraid to let go. You're afraid to lose them. And while everyone hesitates, your fortified growth remains buried under rubble.

> *You cannot* WIN *the war for top talent while defending the debris.*

A scalable culture of fortified growth, innovation, and retention depends on one discipline: digging in the right strategic places.

You must:

- Uncover the buried assumptions
- Confront the inherited dysfunction
- Disrupt the "we've always done it this way" mindset in the strategic areas that undermine forward motion

The role of leadership is not to preserve comfort—it's to fortify the future.

Fortification starts with strategic excavation.

Don't rush to build. Don't paper over the cracks.

Uncover your foundation. Clear the rubble. Then—and only then—can you fortify your growth.

Ask yourself—"What must be removed in my company or culture before scalable growth can be fortified?" The answer to that question is the door to a future that scales through sustainable growth. But clearing the rubble is only half the battle—some debris is visible, and some is hidden. That's where the second challenge emerges.

The role of leadership is not to preserve comfort—it's to protect the future.

Without the king's backing, Nehemiah's fortification efforts would've failed under

Tobiah's resistance. Passion may spark momentum—but his success required authority, resources, and support beyond himself. Power and support turn momentum into movement.

So, here's one of the toughest questions every leader must face: Will you cling to sacred rubble just to keep the peace, or will you choose to fortify your growth?

The moment you choose fortification over comfort; three unavoidable barriers rise in your path. Each one must be exposed, confronted, and cleared—or your growth stops before it starts. Now let's break them open.

FIRST: ELIMINATE GENERATIONAL CONFLICT

Let's start by naming the elephant in the room:

Generational conflict is real— and it's draining your organization of time, talent, and revenue.

Here's what most leaders overlook: It doesn't have to be this way.

I've seen generational tension quietly and loudly erode high-performing teams, fracture communication, overwhelm seasoned leaders, and push your best young talent straight out the door. In nearly every case, leaders try to "ride it out," hoping the tension will dissolve on its own.

It never does. And by the time they speak up, it's already too late.

This conflict isn't unique to one industry or one company—it's universal. It appears in every sector, every region, and every organizational structure I've studied. Its prevalence is so significant that it reveals itself immediately in the first question I ask in my research:

"What's the first word that comes to mind when you think of the younger workforce?"

Pause and answer the question yourself.

It's simple— but the responses are alarmingly consistent.

After surveying **54,000**+ participants across thirty-four nations, the top three responses have remained static for more than a decade. Further, the pattern is reinforced and repeats everywhere:

Every keynote. Every leadership retreat. Every Vistage room. Every boardroom of high-performing executives.

I ask the same question. The answers fire back instantly—confident and deeply revealing.

The top three responses:

> *Entitled. Lazy. Selfish.*

These three words are more than perceptions – they are organizational barriers.

Why should these static responses concern us deeply?

TWO ALARMING REALITIES

First: These responses aren't jokes. They aren't said with a smirk, sarcasm, or even hesitation.

They're delivered with conviction—real observations rooted in real experiences. And here's the alarming part:

They haven't changed in more than a decade.

Not even as younger employees have matured, advanced, and proven themselves essential to organizational growth.

I've watched these static perceptions create dysfunctional behavioral patterns that blind leaders, weaken trust, and quietly hold companies—many with extraordinary products, services, and talent—back from their full potential.

Second: You cannot fortify or build a thriving organization on a foundation of distrust and disdain. When leaders operate from distrust, they unintentionally absorb responsibilities that belong to others—creating unnecessary stress, burnout, and frustration. I've seen seasoned executives and managers carrying the weight of junior staff not because of capability, but because of a lack of trust.

That is not a performance issue. It's a cultural issue, a leadership wellness issue, and ultimately, a revenue issue.

Clarity about expectations, roles, and growth is what breaks this distrust cycle.

THE OPPORTUNITY

Generational conflict inside your building isn't a permanent condition—but it is a direct threat to growth, culture, and retention. The good news is, it's absolutely solvable.

You will not eliminate generational tension by ignoring it, tiptoeing around it, or hoping it fades with time.

You eliminate it with CLARITY. When clarity is reinforced by active accountability, it becomes the currency that permanently breaks the grip of generational conflict inside the company.

A clearly defined path of growth and success for every employee—rooted in informed, tested, practical application—is the only proven way to bridge the divide.

This is where true multi-generational alignment begins—and where your organization gains its competitive advantage.

When this path is in place:

- Trust is rebuilt across generational lines.
- Younger employees are equipped and empowered to deliver results.
- Leaders are freed to lead strategically, not reactively.
- Culture shifts from frustration to alignment.
- Retention rises. Innovation grows. And momentum returns.

This is not theory. It's a reality I've witnessed time and again in companies that choose to lead with clarity instead of assumption.

Generational conflict isn't a problem—it's an invitation. An invitation to lead better. To trust smarter. To grow together.

And the first step? Define the path—and walk it together.

NOW, LET'S ASK THE YOUNGER WORKFORCE

When Millennials and Gen Z are asked the exact same question—"What's the first word that comes to mind when you think of your own generation?"—their responses have also remained consistent:

> *Creative. Collaborative. Smart.*

And just like that, the generational gap becomes glaring.

On one side: entitled, lazy, selfish. On the other, the self-perception: creative, collaborative, smart.

That's the generational divide playing out daily— on Zoom calls, in strategy sessions, during performance reviews, and across every department. And the tension is real.

Leaders think: "If you're so creative, why do you act entitled?"

Employees think: "If I'm capable and driven, why don't you believe in me?"

This is the tension—but it's not a dead end, it's our leadership opportunity.

Both perceptions are valid—and leadership must address both. Many leaders have witnessed entitled behavior. But they've also seen flashes of brilliance, innovation, and grit. The key isn't choosing one truth over another—it's learning how to lead both truths toward a better outcome.

What if we could close the gap—not by compromising standards, but by activating potential? What if we stopped asking, "How do we fix them?" and started asking, "How do we lead them?"

The future belongs to the organizations that bridge this gap—not with slogans or programs, but with real strategy, true presence, and earned trust. Because every generation has its flaws, but every generation also has its genius. If we want to WIN the talent war, we must learn to see both—and lead accordingly.

What if we could channel the energy of a creative, collaborative, and smart workforce into measurable impact—through structure, through trust, and through presence?

We must.

It begins with leaders who are bold enough to build what's missing: A clearly defined path of growth and success.

This is your invitation to eliminate generational conflict.

SECOND, OPEN THE ACCOUNTABILITY GATE TO SUSTAINABLE GROWTH

Let's make it simple:

There is one gate to sustainable growth with the younger workforce—and it's not compensation. It's not flexibility. It's not perks.

Active accountability is the driver behind attracting, engaging, and retaining the best talent represented in the younger generations. Active accountability is the gate every company must open to achieve sustainable growth with today's workforce.

And if those lines surprised you—you're in good company. They shocked me, too.

For years, I wrestled with one simple but pressing question:

What is the most critical step that leaders must take to WIN the talent war?

I struggled to figure it out. I'd seen companies led by experienced, responsible executives—leaders who owned the P&L, drove strategic growth, cared about their teams, and often lived by the mantra: "The buck stops here." Still, they were struggling. Despite every good intention, generational tension was hurting morale, fluidity, innovation—and employee retention.

I've had the unique privilege of being invited into organizations of every size, sector, and culture to observe their challenges up close. And time after time, when those leaders reach out in their moments of deep frustration, they're searching for practical solutions to position their companies for sustainable growth with the younger generation.

Across all those conversations, one statement carries the greatest weight of fear and frustration:

"I'm fearful they will quit if I hold them accountable."

After hearing leaders echo that statement for several years, it hit me. The issue wasn't talent. It wasn't mission. It wasn't even culture.

It was accountability.

ACTIVE ACCOUNTABILITY – THE SINGLE GATE TO SUSTAINABLE GROWTH

If you seek to WIN the talent war with the younger workforce, accountability is not optional —it's the gate you must pass through.

The truth leaders confront is this:

accountability has become a point of fear for many leaders. They worry:

- If I hold them accountable, they'll quit.
- If I press too hard, I'll lose them.
- Replacing them is costly. Disruption is even worse.

So, what do many leaders do?

They ease up—they begin to lead from a place of timidity, not authority. They compromise their standards. They quietly dilute expectations. They let the culture slip... just to keep people from walking out the door.

But that strategy doesn't WIN loyalty. It doesn't drive performance. And it certainly doesn't build growth.

WHY ACCOUNTABILITY CAN'T BE OPTIONAL

Core values and mission statements look great on the wall, but without active accountability, they're just decoration. Remove accountability and the mission becomes noise—and the organization loses its edge, its trust, and its integrity.

Where accountability fades, companies don't just stall—they decline.

Which is why I encourage leaders to do something bold and countercultural:

Inflate accountability.

Don't suppress it. Don't soften it.

Elevate it.

REDEFINING ACCOUNTABILITY: FROM HIERARCHY TO RECIPROCITY

Here's where the generational shift gets fascinating.

In my mind, the definition of accountability is absolute - it always followed a clear, top-down structure. Executives hold senior leaders accountable. Senior leaders hold managers accountable. Managers hold frontline employees accountable. It's the unquestionable age-old paradigm that organizational leaders have trusted and utilized as a source of growth.

But today's younger workforce rejects that model— which kept me rooted in entitled, lazy, and selfish perspectives for several years. I couldn't understand how anyone could reject the absolute model of accountability!

Until I understood what they were asking for:

Not less accountability.

Reciprocal accountability.

Metrics in my research and hundreds of conversations with members of the younger workforce substantiate that they want to be held accountable. They want to be held to high standards.

But here's the seismic shift in organizational history: the younger workforce is now firmly and fearlessly holding you accountable as their leader.

> *The younger workforce wants you to hold them accountable! But... they are also holding you accountable!*

Know this with confidence: it's not rebellion—it's a committed desire to grow and succeed. They are seeking to build their life and career within a leadership culture built on reciprocal accountability.

THE NEW REALITY: RECIPROCAL ACCOUNTABILITY

Here's what's happening inside your company right now, whether you realize it or not:

Young employees are holding you accountable for delivering a clear, structured path of growth and success—not scattershot direction, not guesswork from a compass, but intentional clarity.

No employee ever joined a company thinking, "In one year I'll quit." Top talent doesn't sign on just for a paycheck—they sign on because they believe in your mission, they believe in your leadership, and they see the potential for a future.

But when they can't see a path forward—or the path feels vague, inconsistent, or random—they lose direction. And in today's workforce reality, when high-potential people don't receive a map and feel lost, they don't wait... they leave.

This is why some of your many talented young employees walk away after twelve-eighteen months, even if they started with fire in their eyes. They weren't handed a roadmap—they were handed a compass and told to figure it out.

But here's the flip side: when they do have that roadmap, when they see what growth looks like and how they get there, they don't just stay— they thrive. And so does your business.

Because every time a young employee achieves a step forward in their growth, your organization benefits.

So, what is the younger workforce holding you accountable for? A clearly defined path of growth and success.

THE EFFECTIVE MODEL OF ACCOUNTABILITY MOVING FORWARD

Accountability begins with leadership. It flows through every employee, guided by a clearly defined path of growth and success. And it returns to the leader—measured in follow-through, trust, and outcomes.

This is reciprocal accountability: owned by leaders, carried by the system, proven in results.

LET ME BE CLEAR: LET THEM WALK

Before we dive into the critical components of a clearly defined path of growth and success, we need to pause and address a foundational principle of reciprocal accountability.

Once your path is in place—and you've implemented it with consistency—it's time to set clear expectations. Every employee, especially those in the younger workforce, must be held accountable for their productivity, behavior, and responsibilities. If they resist accountability, let them walk.

> *Timid or watered-down accountability destroys organizations.*

When leaders avoid conflict in the name of retention, it only creates a deeper dysfunction.

The single most essential attribute of high performing, growing organizations is active accountability. And it must apply to everyone—regardless of age, role, or seniority.

If someone refuses to be held accountable, keeping them guarantees organization damage, regardless of their role.

Let them walk.

Accountability is not negotiable.

I CAN'T SURVIVE WITHOUT THAT EMPLOYEE!

When I tell leaders they must "let people walk" when they refuse accountability, the pushback is consistently the same:

> *"You don't understand... we can't survive without that employee."*

If that's where you find yourself, let me take you to an experience that revealed a hard truth: sometimes what you think you can't live without is the very thing contaminating your entire system.

I lived in the Caribbean for twenty-two years, with the last eleven on the island of St. John. Although St. John is one of the most affluent islands in the region, it has one major challenge: there is no natural water source. Not a river. Not a spring. Nothing.

Whether you live in a $20-million villa or a small hillside cottage like we did, every drop of water must be caught from your roof and stored in a cistern beneath your home. For seven months of the year, rain is plentiful. But during the five-month dry season, water becomes precious—and many people's cisterns run dry.

When that happens, you rely on a small fleet of water trucks that haul desalinated water across the island. But during dry season, demand far exceeds supply, and waiting two weeks for a delivery is normal.

One dry season, our cistern ran out of water. After two weeks of waiting, a truck finally came and refilled our cistern. That night I jumped into the shower—only to notice the water smelled foul. Then, as I brushed my teeth, the taste confirmed something was wrong. I went to the cistern, opened the heavy lid, and froze.

A large dead iguana was floating on top of our water supply.

The dry season had pushed not just humans, but animals, to desperation. This iguana had found a narrow opening, slipped into the cistern seeking relief, and drowned.

Now I had a dilemma—one that demanded an immediate decision.

I had three choices:

- Leave the dead iguana and treat the water.
- Remove the iguana and treat the water.
- Remove the iguana, drain the cistern, clean it, and start over.

Draining the tank felt unthinkable. I believed I couldn't survive another day without water.

But keeping it—even treated—meant one thing: I'd be masking toxic water. And toxic water, no matter how well you filter it, still makes your family sick.

Because I concluded that I could not survive another day without water, draining the water felt unthinkable. But keeping it—even treated—meant one thing: I'd be masking toxic water. And toxic water, no matter how well you filter it, still makes your family sick.

There was only one real option: Remove the iguana. Drain the cistern. Clean it. And wait for fresh water.

It was the only way to restore health.

LEADERSHIP APPLICATION: REMOVING THE "IGUANAS" THAT CONTAMINATE CULTURE

Every organization has a cistern—its culture. It's where people draw their energy, clarity, direction, and trust. And just like my water supply, that culture is either clean and life-giving… or silently contaminated.

The strategical truth is this: Most leaders know there is a dead iguana floating in their cultural cistern. However, in an effort to keep the employee happy and in the building, they leave the iguana in the cistern and desperately try to decontaminate the water.

It might be…

- A toxic attitude that's been tolerated for too long
- A confusing or inconsistent path of growth
- A supervisor who leads through fear instead of clarity
- An untouchable high performer who poisons the team
- A lack of active accountability

- A hidden conflict no one wants to address
- An outdated mindset that chokes innovation

And leaders convince themselves that if they just treat the water—send an email, do a training, host a meeting—the problem will fix itself.

But treating toxic water never makes it healthy.

The only way to restore organizational health is the same way I restored my home's water supply: You identify the contamination. You remove it. You clean the cistern. And you rebuild with clarity and intention.

Clarity always demands this kind of decision: remove the source—not just treat the symptoms.

In practical terms, this may mean exiting a toxic high-performer, restructuring a misaligned role, or sunsetting a beloved but outdated process.

It's inconvenient. It's uncomfortable. But it is the only path to sustainable growth.

You cannot attract, engage, or retain top talent if your cultural cistern is contaminated. Your best people will taste the toxicity long before you do—and they will quietly leave in search of clean water.

The **3** WINS journey starts here—with clarity about what must stay and what must go: Eliminate the hidden impediments. Clean the cistern. Build a culture worth staying for.

The pathway to sustainable growth is not found in treating contaminated culture—it's found in removing what's poisoning it.

Here's what I'm asking you to do:

- Make accountability active. Don't leave it vague. Make it part of everyday conversations, expectations, and feedback.
- Model the culture. You hold them accountable, be accountable to them by providing a clearly defined path of growth and success.
- Let go when needed. If an employee refuses accountability—regardless of age, seniority or generation—let them walk.

The younger workforce doesn't fear accountability. They crave it. They want to be challenged. They want to grow.

They want to trust the people leading them—and they want to become the kind of people worth following.

It's time we give them that chance.

With clarity. With courage. With accountability.

THIRD: CLARIFY THE TRUTH ABOUT THE "THREAT" YOUNGER GENERATIONS POSE

DISMANTLING THE "THREAT" NARRATIVE

Here's a powerful and sobering stat from my research:

64%

---

of leaders believe the younger workforce is a threat to their organizational health.

When leaders perceive their workforce as a threat, they lead with defensiveness. They build walls instead of bridges. They create tension instead of trust. When we view younger employees as a threat, that belief inevitably shapes our culture into one defined by fear and resistance.

It's time to allow facts to dismantle that destructive mindset—not because younger generations are perfect, but because they are not the enemy. They are your future.

Our job as leaders isn't to control that future—it's to prepare it. To create environments where creativity, ambition, intelligence, collaboration and innovation can thrive. Especially among the very employees who will soon lead us forward.

THE MISINFORMATION TRAP: IS THE YOUNGER WORKFORCE A THREAT—OR OUR GREATEST OPPORTUNITY?

We're drowning in opinions about the younger generations throughout our society. Open any article, scroll through any feed, and you'll find a tidal wave of advice, insights, and warnings about the younger workforce. Much of it is outdated, inaccurate, or flat-out false. And when leaders build cultures or make decisions based on misinformation or unchallenged assumptions, the results are predictable—frustration, disengagement, and the loss of the very talent we're desperate to keep. Those firsthand experiences breed a mindset of fear—and when leaders operate from fear, they unintentionally create a culture of threat, not trust.

Let's stop pretending: a strong brand, a great product, and a seasoned team no longer guarantee success. In today's workforce war, reputation doesn't recruit. Perks don't retain. And charisma doesn't build cultures that last.

King Solomon nailed it: "If it costs you everything, get understanding." That's not poetic—it's strategic. Because if you're building your leadership approach on assumptions, emotions, or recycled headlines, you're not leading—you're guessing. And guessing is expensive. It drains budgets, erodes trust, and cripples momentum.

Chasing popular voices or viral workplace trends doesn't solve your retention crisis. It just delays the fallout.

If you want to WIN, prepare like it.

That starts with clearing out the clutter.

Strip away the assumptions. Get understanding. Challenge what you think you know. Trade reaction for revelation.

Because clarity isn't a luxury—it's a weapon.

To build a path of growth and success that actually works, you must reject assumption and embrace the truths that define today's younger workforce. Not wishful thinking. Not outdated stereotypes.

Truth.

Your perception of the younger workforce will either be your competitive advantage or your greatest liability. To gain insight—not noise—

we're going to unpack five misunderstood areas of behavior. These aren't trends. They're truths. And they help you understand if the younger generations are a threat or opportunity to your company:

- Core Values
- Job Migration
- Work Location
- Financial Position
- Organizational Mindset

1. CORE VALUES: A CLASH OR A CALL?

When senior leaders are asked if the younger generations share their values, **78%** say NO– that Zillennials' values are misguided.

Now, flip the script.

When Zillennials are asked if they respect and adhere to the core values of older generations, **71%** say YES.

When asked if they value leadership wisdom from the generations before them, **76%** said they do.

That's not rejection–it's a cry for guidance. What we're witnessing isn't a dismissal of long-held values–it's a desire for structure and mentorship that simply doesn't exist in most organizations.

Don't get snared by the noise. Many "news" outlets portray younger generations as anarchists rejecting everything that made previous generations strong. But, as with every era, it's the extremes that get the attention. Do not project those extremes onto the young people in your building.

The problem isn't a generational difference in values—it's a lack of intentional systems to translate those values into shared purpose. They aren't rejecting values or leadership. They're asking for them.

So, the data forces a simple leadership question: does the desire from younger employees represent a threat to your culture—or an opportunity to strengthen it?

2. JOB MIGRATION: SURELY RETENTION IS A THREAT?

Let's talk tenure.

The average Baby Boomer remains at their respective company **19.1** years. The average GenXer: **10.2** years. The average Millennial: **21** months. The average Gen Z: **11** months.

Let me ask: How long can an organization sustain growth when its largest workforce block is turning over, on average, every sixteen months?

It can't—and the cost of pretending otherwise is catastrophic to continuity, culture, and revenue.

Without a fundamentally different approach, employee retention is a genuine threat. But it's not an unsolvable one.

> *Turnover is a variable you control.*

Stop leading from assumptions and start building a clearly defined path of growth and success.

This point has been made to me hundreds of times by CEOs who attend my keynotes or reach out for guidance. Consider just four recent examples:

- A CEO of an HVAC company in the Northeast hired **74** employees last year—and lost **72** of them within **12** months.
- A healthcare CEO on the West Coast hires **400** new employees each year hoping to retain just ninety.

- A Southern manufacturing CEO hired **1,540** employees over the last twenty-four months —and lost **1,260** of them.
- The CEO of a CPA firm told me they're losing an average of **30** CPAs every quarter.

These aren't outliers. They're warnings. And the root cause isn't generational flakiness or shifting values. It's organizational ambiguity—a lack of compelling reasons to stay. When clarity is missing, leaders often mistake the consequences of their systems for flaws in their people.

In every one of these cases, what's missing is a documented step-by-step path of growth and success—a clarity gap, not a character gap.

Here's the good news: turnover is not an inevitable threat. You control both the outcome and the opportunity.

And as we move forward in this book, we're going to unpack the informed, tested, and practical solutions that will allow you to end this cycle for good—and build a workforce designed for sustainable growth.

So based on the data, is Job Migration a threat to your culture—or an opportunity to strengthen it?

3. WORK LOCATION: A RETURN TO COMMUNITY

There's a popular narrative: "Young employees don't want to come back to the office." But the data (facts) tells a very different story.

Among today's Zillennials:

- **47%** prefer working exclusively on-site (compared to **52%** of Boomers/Gen X)
- **52%** prefer hybrid or flexible models (compared to **41%** Boomers/Gen X)
- Remote-only preferences are rapidly declining across all ages

So, what's the real opportunity? A renewed recognition that human connection is not optional—it's essential to performance, trust, and well-being.

Older and younger workers are not diverging on this issue; they're converging. We thrive in connection and community. Hybrid work isn't rising because younger generations are resistant or disengaged. It's rising because, when designed well, it reflects how people actually do their best work.

And this is where leadership matters.

Effective, productive workplaces are built on strong interpersonal relationships. The younger workforce understands this—and they are actively evaluating leaders on whether they create the structures that make real connection possible.

So based on the data, Remote and Hybrid work present a simple leadership question: is this a threat to your culture—or an opportunity to strengthen it?

4. FINANCIAL POWER: THE CONSUMER IS ALREADY HERE—THE DECISION MAKER IS COMING FAST

Before we begin: when we talk about financial positioning in this section, we are talking about Millennials—not Gen Z. Gen Z is still early in their financial lifecycle, and the long-term trends aren't fully formed yet.

However, this isn't just about your employees' financial reality. Millennial financial power is shaping your workforce and your customer base. Ignoring this shift puts both at risk.

The research exposes a powerful correlation—one that directly impacts your P&L.

Organizations that excel in attracting, engaging, and retaining younger employees are also excelling at converting them into clients.

The inverse is just as clear—if you're struggling to connect with younger talent internally, you're likely failing to capture them externally as customers.

Bottom line:

If you lose them inside your company, you're probably losing them outside it as well.

So why does that matter? Let's look at the numbers:

- Millennials currently hold the highest annual purchasing power of any generation. (US Census Bureau)
- Millennials alone are on track to inherit **$68 trillion**. When Gen Z is included, the number climbs to **$124 trillion**—the greatest transfer of wealth ever recorded (U.S. Federal Reserve)
- Millennials carry **42%** less credit card debt and **32%** lower mortgage balances than previous generations at the same age (U.S. Federal Reserve)
- **79%** of Millennials have at least three months of emergency savings—virtually tied with Baby Boomers
- The Federal Reserve identifies Millennials as the most frugal generation since WWII

This isn't a reckless generation—it's a financially disciplined one. They're stepping into financial control, both as consumers and as corporate decision-makers. And the shift is coming fast: By 2030, **83-86%** of all CFOs will be Millennials.

This makes Millennial financial power one of the greatest competitive opportunities business leaders will experience in their lifetime.

Yet despite this reality, **64%** of seasoned leaders still view them as a threat.

That mindset isn't just outdated—it's expensive.

So based on the data, the Financial Position of Millennials presents a critical leadership question: is this a threat to your culture—or an opportunity to strengthen it?

5. THE REAL "THREAT": STRUCTURAL DISRUPTION

So... if Zillennials aren't the actual threat to our sustainable growth, what is?

It's this:

The younger workforce is challenging structures that we resolutely assumed were absolute. From accountability models to leadership hierarchies, from financial systems to work definitions—they're rethinking everything.

Although this shift may challenge or threaten leaders shaped by traditional structures, it's exactly what enables Millennials to emerge as one of the most efficient and transformative generations in modern organizational history.

In fact, as a Baby Boomer, I believe this so strongly—based on the outcomes of my research and implementation work—that I originally titled my first book: Millennials: The Greatest Generation in Organizational History.

(My former publisher, whose board was made up entirely of Baby Boomers, quickly rejected the title. But I stand by it.)

OPPORTUNITY OR OBSTACLE?

Change is uncomfortable—especially when it disrupts what once worked effectively. But a generation that challenges the norm isn't disloyal; it's catalytic. Yes, they question. Yes, they push back. Yes, it's frustrating and can even feel insulting—but that tension is a catalyst for innovation and growth.

So, ask yourself: Are you resisting what you don't understand—or ready to act on what others continue to ignore?

This is your moment. Choose action.

Engage them with clarity, structure, and trust—and you don't just calm a perceived threat; you unlock unprecedented growth.

Millennials and Gen Z aren't your obstacle. They're your competitive edge—if you lead them well.

The question isn't whether they're different. The question is whether you will lead with facts or with fear.

If you don't define their path, they'll define it without you. And if they can't see a future with you, they'll stop building one.

Clarity WINS. Structure scales. Direction retains.

This generation isn't a threat; they're the greatest growth opportunity of your lifetime—if you have the courage to leverage their strengths.

Lead What's Next — Final Charge: Clarity Is the New Leadership Currency. Stop Guessing. Start Leading.

Leaders who invest in clarity don't just hold onto their best people—they unleash them.

Clarity isn't convenient. It requires tough conversations, courageous transparency, and relentless follow-through. You can't fake it. You can't outsource it. You can't delay it.

Your next move will either solidify your culture or fracture it. Are you ready to give your people what they've been silently begging for? A defined path. A reason to stay. The next chapter shows you how to build that path and start winning the war for talent.

We'll begin with WIN **#1**—how to WIN Talent by building an irresistible map of growth and success that top performers can see, trust, and follow.

QUICK AUDIT PRIOR TO CREATING THE PATH OF CLARITY:

Ask yourself—and your leadership team:

- Do our employees know what success looks like here?
- Is there a defined, documented path from entry to growth?
- Are our expectations clear, our feedback consistent, and our rewards aligned with progress?
- If we change nothing, what does that cost us —in talent, time, and revenue?

Now pause for a moment and consider the larger implication.

The first strand of the **3** WINS Operating System is clarity.

But clarity alone does not attract talent.

Clarity must become visible.

That visibility is what turns leadership intention into a system people can follow.

It's time to build the MAP.

If you're unsure where to start, I'll walk you through step by step, with a few non-negotiables that must be active.

Step by step. WIN by WIN.

Now let's build the path that drives growth—and secures your organization's future.

Clarity defines the path. But clarity must become visible if it is going to attract talent.

The moment clarity becomes visible; the **3** WINS Operating System begins to activate.

In the next chapter, we build the map that makes growth visible—turning clarity into momentum.

READ THIS BEFORE YOU BLAME THE NEXT GENERATION

CHAPTER 4

WIN Talent: Make Growth Visible

Create a Culture Talent Can't Resist

In Chapter 3 we established the foundation of the **3** WINS Operating System: clarity.

But clarity alone is not enough.

If people cannot see the path of growth, clarity remains theory.

In this chapter we turn clarity into something visible—a map of growth that attracts the talent your organization needs to win.

THE PROBLEM ISN'T TALENT — IT'S DIRECTION

STABILITY, PAY, AND PRESTIGE STILL MATTER —but the next generation of top talent is no longer choosing employers through those filters. They're choosing clarity.

Organizations that provide a clearly defined path of growth pull exceptional performers out of the market with magnetic force, while everyone else watches their pipelines collapse and their cultures fracture. The greatest competitive edge in today's economy isn't technology, capital, or strategy—its talent anchored to a visible, undeniable map of growth and success. Companies that build this map will accelerate. Those that don't will be outpaced, out-innovated, and outgrown by leaders who understand one simple truth: the future belongs to organizations that show people exactly where they're going.

WIN talent is the first of the **3** WINS—because without the right people coming in and staying in, nothing else in your growth strategy can scale.

THE LEADERSHIP GAP: COMPASS THINKING VS. MAP EXPECTATIONS

For decades, older generations—Baby Boomers and Gen X, what I refer to collectively as BXers—built their careers with a compass in hand. Direction was vague, the path was broad, and success was expected to unfold over time.

After almost every keynote, CEOs pull me aside and ask the same question:

"What's the most fundamental difference between the older and younger workforce?"

They ask it through the lens of performance, accountability, and retention.

Here's the answer:

> *Seasoned leaders are confident navigating their career with a compass. Younger employees are rejecting the compass– they're looking for a map.*

A compass provides general direction. A map provides clarity, milestones, and momentum.

The age-old message from employers has been simple: Head north, stay the course, and success will follow. And for generations it has been an effective method of growth and success. Stability was the norm. Change was predictable. The compass was enough.

But that era is over.

Today's younger workforce—Millennials and Gen Z— are navigating a completely different landscape: one defined by rapid change, digital noise, constant disruption, and overwhelming choice.

To hand them a compass and say "just head that way" is not guidance—it's negligence.

They don't want vague direction—they're looking for a clearly defined map. A map with milestones, purpose, feedback, and outcomes.

Without it, they wander. They disengage. They leave. And when they leave, they take your momentum, innovation, and future growth with them.

The cost of not having a clearly defined path of growth isn't just turnover— it's organizational erosion.

Here's your question:

When you're onboarding a new employee, are you handing them a compass or a clearly defined map?

The answer to that question has a far-reaching impact: employee engagement, retention, market leverage, and innovation; all of which drive revenue. It's time to stop handing out compasses that we conveniently call onboarding. Start handing new employees a map.

WHY THE COMPASS FAILED—AND WHY THE WORKFORCE NOW REQUIRES A MAP

Today's young professionals are not asking for coddling; they are operating within a different economic and cultural reality. They entered the workforce during volatility—digital acceleration, remote disruption, public layoffs, and constant visibility into organizational instability.

From a front-row seat, they watched previous generations pursue success at significant personal cost: burnout normalized, imbalance rewarded, and endurance mistaken for excellence.

They are not rejecting achievement from the generations that preceded them; they are rejecting the ambiguity in the path of achievement.

The compass model assumed directional stability in a predictable environment. That environment no longer exists.

What this generation is asking for is not less challenge, but more clarity—defined milestones, visible progression, and structured advancement. In short: a map.

Leaders who continue to rely on directional ambiguity will experience attrition. Leaders who replace it with defined pathways will experience acceleration.

THE CAMINO REVELATION

While hiking the Camino de Santiago across Spain, I watched this generational metaphor unfold in real time.

Young hikers followed their GPS with total confidence. Older pilgrims like me were certain that if we simply kept walking west, we would eventually reach our destination.

From my Baby Boomer perspective, watching them stare at their phones and be guided by screens felt infuriating.

I kept asking myself: why travel across one of the most extraordinary routes on the planet only to stay glued to a screen?

In my mind, they were missing the richness of the journey.

But here's the part I didn't expect: My "trust the compass" approach caused me to get lost—twice. Both times, I trudged into the next town well after dark, hungry, exhausted, and missing the fellowship with other pilgrims. And, for some twisted reason, I wore that off-beat detour like a badge of honor.

Even though we all ended each day in the same town, they arrived hours before I did. I was frustrated that they were blowing past the

Roman-built cathedrals, ancient monasteries, and centuries-old landmarks along the way—but they were energized by something I completely overlooked: their efficiency, their momentum, and the deep community they were building together from town to town.

It took me weeks to see what was right in front of me:

> *My compass gave me history. Their map gave them community.*

And that's when the truth landed:

The older generation values the journey. The younger generation values the connection.

Both are right— but only one arrives with a tribe.

WHEN THERE IS NO MAP, PEOPLE DRIFT

In my research, **68%** of younger employees say their employer offers no clearly defined path for growth and success. That's not a missed opportunity—it's a leadership failure. A clear path is the dividing line between thriving teams and stalled-out cultures.

It fuels engagement, loyalty, and forward momentum. Without it? Confusion, frustration, and quiet quitting take over.

If you're serious about winning the talent war, start with this blunt question:

Can your team see the road ahead—or are you expecting them to navigate a maze you never mapped out?

Here's the danger: When you leave blanks, they will fill them—with their own expectations, priorities, and timelines. And odds are, those don't align with yours.

The result? Frustration. Disappointment. And preventable turnover.

If you don't define the path with informed, tested, practical solutions, you can't control the outcome.

> *Build the map—or lose your people to someone who will.*

A MAP IS YOUR MOST POWERFUL RECRUITMENT TOOL

Top organizations aren't winning talent with signing bonuses—they're winning with clarity. Today's workforce isn't afraid of responsibility. They're fed up with ambiguity. They're not running from hard work. They're running from leaders who can't define the destination.

Recruit with a map, not a promise. When you give people direction, they don't just show up—they demonstrate the depth of their capability.

THE MAP IS NOT THE EASY WAY – IT'S THE RIGHT WAY

A clearly defined path of growth and success isn't supposed to be smooth—it's supposed to be stretching. Challenges and tests aren't roadblocks—they're engineered requirements.

But too many leaders operate from fear—afraid that accountability will scare younger employees away. That fear produces sensitivity instead of intensity. It coddles instead of cultivates.

The misunderstanding is this:

Shielding your people from challenges and intensity doesn't protect them—it weakens them.

If you want resilient, high-performing teams, then build challenge into the path.

Let them be tested. Let them struggle. Let them rise.

Resilience isn't given—it's earned. And growth is never forged in comfort—it's forged in challenge.

REAL TALK: WE DID THIS

We built the bubble. Boomers and Gen X softened the edges, cleared the obstacles, and handed out participation trophies—then wondered why the next generation expects support.

We removed the struggle and called it love, and now we complain they can't handle adversity.

Let's own it—this is our doing.

But here's reality: They can handle adversity. What they've lacked is the opportunity to face it without being rescued. As leaders, our job isn't to clear the path—it's to prepare them for it.

Not with comfort. Not with coddling. With clarity, challenge, and coaching.

The next generation doesn't need protection —they need permission to struggle, the space to fight, and the expectation to rise.

Stop softening the blow and start building the backbone.

ACTION STEP: STOP GUESSING – START BUILDING

Audit your organization right now.

Are you handing out vague compasses—or are you building clear, actionable maps?

If it's the former, it's time to shift—fast. Define the path. Mark the milestones. Build in challenges.

Provide direction with precision—not just encouragement with fluff. Because here's the good news:

When younger employees can see the road ahead, they don't just walk—they accelerate. But if they're left to guess, they'll leave.

Clarity drives confidence. Build the map—or lose the momentum.

Lead What's Next — Final Charge: Build the Map. Show the Way. Keep the Talent.

Your people aren't asking for perfection. They're not asking for more perks, more pay, or more hollow promises. They're asking for one thing: direction. And if you don't give them a clear, visible map of growth, they will wander—or worse, they will leave.

This is not the era of the compass. That era—where vague direction and patience was enough—is over. Today's workforce needs mile markers, milestones, and a mission that feels alive in their hands. They need to see that their journey here leads somewhere worth staying for.

But a map alone does not win the war for talent.

The organizations that attract the strongest people are the ones where that map is visible, active, and producing growth.

In the next chapter we install the first outcome of the **3** WINS Operating System:

WIN #**1** – ATTRACT.

But a MAP is only as strong as the leader who delivers it. Chapter 5 introduces the leadership behaviors that turn your MAP into movement.

CHAPTER 5

WIN #1:

Attract

Clarity Makes Growth Visible—And Talent Comes to You.

YOU WON'T WIN THE WAR FOR TALENT by posting more jobs, offering bigger bonuses, or filling seats faster. You WIN it by embracing one unshakable truth:

WIN **#1** is WIN Talent—what we call ATTRACT.

WIN **#1** is simple: when growth is visible, talent comes to you—predicably.

From here forward, you'll install the **3** WINS Operating System:

- WIN **#1** - Attract
- WIN **#2** - Engage
- WIN - Retain 3

TO ATTRACT THE RIGHT PEOPLE—the people who stay, grow, and elevate your culture—you must start by confronting a few Leadership Realities.

> *Talent doesn't follow enthusiasm.*
> *Talent follows maps.*

LEADERSHIP REALITY #1: "FILLING THE POSITION" IS AN OBSOLETE STRATEGY.

For generations, leadership followed a familiar script: Someone leaves → post the job → fill the role → move on.

It worked because tenure worked:

- Boomers stayed **19.1** years
- Gen X stayed **10.2** years

Refilling positions felt like progress—because, for decades, it was. But today? That math exposes a different reality.

Millennials stay **21** months.

Gen Z stays **11** months.

Combined, your largest workforce block gives you **16** months—barely enough time to train them before the countdown resets.

So, if your hiring strategy is simply to "fill the position," here's what you're actually doing:

Restarting the turnover clock every **16** months.

And each restart drains your organization more than the last:

- Higher training costs
- Lost momentum and stalled initiatives
- Cultural fatigue and constant goodbyes
- Teams watching the revolving door spin faster each year

This isn't a talent strategy. It's a retention crisis disguised as progress. A treadmill of rehiring, retraining, and rebuilding—a system engineered for burnout and failure.

The problem isn't that the system is outdated. The problem is that it's unsustainable.

And leaders who cling to it aren't just losing talent—they're losing time, money, culture, and competitive advantage.

The consequences of an obsolete strategy show up in the only place that matters—your people's lived experience.

When the strategy is outdated, the employee experience inevitably follows.

LEADERSHIP REALITY #2

Your talent problem isn't caused by a shrinking labor pool.

It isn't because Millennials or Gen Z are "entitled," "unmotivated," or allergic to hard work.

It's not even about HR needing to post better job ads.

Those explanations are convenient. They're also wrong.

The real issue is far more uncomfortable:

Your younger employees aren't thriving.

And when they're not thriving, they don't stay. And when they don't stay, they certainly don't attract anyone else to your company.

The talent pool isn't shrinking—it's expanding.

But talent no longer flows automatically to the biggest brands.

When the executive team of a Fortune 100 company invited me in to help reverse their workforce trend, the CHRO shared a startling shift.

> *"Before the COVID pandemic," she said, "for every job opening we received an average of* **50** *applicants."*

That meant every hire came from a deep pool of talent—the very best candidates rising to the top.

Today the math tells a very different story.

For every open position, they schedule roughly **25** interviews. Yet on average, only **2.8** candidates actually show up.

Let that sink in.

One of the most recognizable brands in the world—an organization with global visibility, massive resources, and decades of brand equity—is struggling to attract people to an interview.

Collectively, the executive team blamed the no-shows on the behavioral patterns of an "entitled younger workforce."

But what they failed to recognize was something far more revealing: the story their structure was telling in the talent market had become obsolete.

Their message was still centered on the paycheck—with little mention of meaning, purpose, or a clearly defined path of growth.

This isn't a labor shortage.

It's a talent-flow problem.

For decades, the best talent flowed to the biggest brands.

Today the younger workforce is drawn somewhere else entirely:

The company where they believe they will grow.

Brand is no longer the filter.

Growth is.

And the competition for that talent is accelerating faster than most leaders realize.

As Boomers exit the workforce at record speed and U.S. population growth plateaus, the Bureau of Labor Statistics projects **1.2 million** new job openings every year for the next decade.

More openings. Fewer experienced workers. And a fierce battle for high-capacity, high-growth talent.

The organizations that WIN won't be the ones posting more jobs—they'll be the ones where younger employees thrive so visibly, so consistently, that they attract others like magnets.

The war for talent isn't coming—it's already here.

The only question is: Will your culture be a recruiting engine—or a warning sign?

LEADERSHIP REALITY #3

Your ability to attract top talent is no longer dependent on your products and services, but entirely on how your current younger workforce is growing and succeeding.

If they're flourishing—if they can see a clear path to growth, impact, and success—they don't just stay. They talk. They share their experience. They become your loudest advocates and your most powerful recruiters.

But if they're floundering—if they see no future, no purpose, no roadmap—they also talk. Only louder. And what they say drives top talent away before you even get a chance to interview them.

Here's a perspective that can help leaders move forward:

Across more than **54,000** participants in my research, one pattern is unmistakable, your younger workforce is not just filling seats. They are the stories your company is telling in the talent market.

Your best job posting isn't on LinkedIn. It's the lived experience of your younger employees.

Your most effective recruiter isn't HR. It's the passion, progress, and success of your team.

Your biggest draw isn't your mission statement or core values. It's whether or not your younger employees can say, with confidence, "I'm growing here. I'm succeeding here. You should join me."

If they can't say that you've already lost the battle for talent.

LEADERSHIP REALITY #4

You're not just competing against other companies—you're competing against the dreams of the younger generations. If you can't show them how those dreams take root in your organization, you've already lost them.

Millennials and Gen Z want more than a paycheck. They want meaning. And increasingly, they expect that meaning to be woven into the culture they join.

They're not chasing ladder rungs—they're looking for a roadmap. A map that tells them:

- "Here's where you'll grow."
- "Here's who's guiding you."
- "Here's what your impact means."

If they can't see that map? They walk.

But when you give them a tested, clearly defined path of growth and success—and treat retention as revenue—growth becomes predictable.

They stay. They excel. And they recruit.

They become your talent magnet.

The core practice of WIN **#1** is a clearly defined, highly visible path of growth and success for younger employees.

WIN **#1** isn't about how to write a better job ad or tweak your benefits package. It's about creating an environment where your younger workforce grows so visibly and so consistently that top talent is drawn to you long before you ever post a job.

The question isn't whether your younger workforce is telling a story about your culture. The question is:

Is it the story you want told?

One simple question: Are you ready to invest in your people's growth—or are you willing to let your competitors get there first?

And here's the part most leaders overlook: attraction isn't a mystery—it's a measurement. And the data reveals a gap leaders can no longer afford to overlook.

Here's what the numbers make impossible to ignore.

THE BLIND SPOT: OVERFUNDING RECRUITMENT, UNDERVALUING GROWTH

After breaking down HR budgets across hundreds of organizations, one pattern becomes unmistakable:

- **86%** goes to recruiting
- **4%** to employee engagement
- **10%** to retention

That's not just misaligned. It's madness.

It creates a treadmill of chaos: Recruit → Exit → Repeat.

This cycle is financially wasteful and emotionally exhausting. HR teams burn out. Leaders lose trust. Departments lose stability. Cultures lose momentum.

The system isn't just broken. It's consuming itself.

A challenge to every HR director: What percentage of your budget goes toward growing your people versus acquiring new ones?

Warning, you may be shocked by the answer.

You can't spend your way out of a culture problem.

WHAT USED TO WORK NO LONGER WORKS

For decades, employment was anchored to one thing: personal income.

Older generations accepted draining roles because the paycheck fed their families, paid the mortgage, and provided stability. They traded passion for security—and wore that sacrifice like a badge of honor.

Today's workforce sees things differently.

For Millennials and Gen Z, work isn't just about income. It's about outcome. And they're asking bigger questions:

"What impact am I making?"

"Am I becoming someone better because of this role?"

"Am I growing here—or just surviving?"

This isn't laziness or entitlement. It's alignment.

They're not rejecting hard work—they're rejecting wasted years inside cultures that don't grow people, don't value contribution, and don't connect effort to purpose.

Clarity is not optional. It is the first restraint against drift.

Clarity is where leadership begins—but clarity alone is not enough. To hold people together, it must eventually be reinforced by accountability and community.

And here's the uncomfortable truth: They're right.

This shift isn't a threat to leadership—it's an invitation. Because when you create a culture where your younger workforce grows, thrives, and sees their impact, you don't just retain them. You unleash them.

And when they're unleashed—achieving visible, undeniable growth—they become your greatest recruiting asset.

This is where the real work of attraction begins—not with job postings or perks, but with growth, clarity, and purpose woven into the fabric of your culture.

CASE STUDY: CHICK-FIL-A'S PEOPLE-ADVANTAGE

Dan Cathy, CEO of Chick-fil-A, once told me:

> "*McDonald's sells burgers. Starbucks sells coffee. Taco Bell sells tacos. Chick-fil-A sells chicken, but we're in the people business.*"

That philosophy shows up in the numbers. In cities where all four brands compete, Chick-fil-A out-earns McDonald's, Starbucks, and Taco Bell combined in annual revenue—per location.

It's not the chicken. It's the culture.

It's the relentless focus on people development. On clear growth pathways. On consistent coaching.

Want to attract talent? Be obsessed with growing people!

You don't attract talent by selling jobs—you attract talent by showcasing growth.

LEADERSHIP REALITY #5

Growth isn't a perk—it's a partnership.

Who's responsible for growing employees—the individual or the organization?

The answer: both.

Growth is a shared responsibility—a mutual investment and a leadership imperative. I call it a fiduciary responsibility—because when growth fails, so does the future.

This is why I challenge every hiring manager I coach to start interviews with one powerful question:

> "*What are you doing right now to invest in your own personal growth?*"

If a candidate can't answer—if they're doing nothing—then the interview ends there.

It doesn't matter how impressive their résumé looks. Because if they lack the initiative to grow themselves, they won't help grow your company either.

Yes, leaders must provide a clear, intentional pathway for growth—but when either side fails, the outcome is the same: disengagement, turnover, and wasted potential.

Sometimes the clearest truth comes straight from the workforce itself. Case in point: a Millennial named Taylor Gerkin, a member of the

Emerging Leaders structure at Salem One, summed it up perfectly:

> *"If I'm not better at what I do and who I am in six months, I'm in the wrong place."*

That's not entitlement. That's intention—the intention to grow, not just in skill, but in identity. To become stronger in his work and better in his life.

If employees choose not to take a pathway of growth, let them walk. But if no pathway exists, the fault isn't theirs—it's yours. Accountability cuts both ways—employees must choose growth, but leaders must build the path.

The question every leader must answer:

Are you building a culture where growth is the inevitable outcome—or one where the revolving door keeps spinning? One attracts top talent. The other feeds the exit line.

CLIENT CASE STUDY: HOW HRC ENGINEERS, SURVEYORS, AND LANDSCAPE ARCHITECTS WIN TOP TALENT WITHOUT PERKS

How does HRC win the fierce battle for engineers, architects, and surveyors?

They don't show up at job fairs waving pay or benefits packages. They don't lure graduates with signing bonuses or ping-pong tables.

Instead, they send their younger employees—real people living real growth journeys—to talk about the company's clearly defined path of growth and success.

That simple shift WINS the talent war.

Here's the takeaway:

If your leaders can't articulate that same roadmap— in interviews, in onboarding, and in daily interactions—you're already losing ground.

THE ATTRACTION EQUATION: SHINE YOUR LIGHT OR LOSE TOP TALENT

A light isn't meant to stay hidden. It's designed to be placed high—on a stand, on a ceiling—so it fills the entire room.

Your path of growth and success for younger employees works the same way.

If it doesn't exist, you've already lost the talent war. If it exists but stays hidden, it's worthless. But if it's visible—on full display—you don't just compete for talent.

You dominate. You create a magnetic culture that drives sustainable growth and gives you unmatched competitive leverage.

The power to attract top talent comes from one thing: real stories of growth and success from your current employees.

That's the light—and it draws others in.

If you want to WIN, your growth strategy for your people must be visible and undeniable across every touchpoint:

- Careers page
- Job descriptions
- Interview conversations
- Onboarding structure
- Employee testimonials
- Social media presence

If your younger employees aren't posting about how they're growing in your company, your growth structure either doesn't exist—or it doesn't work.

> *You can't attract what you refuse to display.*

Attraction isn't a hiring problem—it's a growth problem.

THE TALENT MAGNET PLAYBOOK: FROM REVOLVING DOOR TO RECRUITING POWERHOUSE

Attraction is a leadership function. Every younger employee on your payroll is broadcasting your organizational reality to the talent market—through the clarity, growth, and momentum they experience under your leadership.

If you want to WIN the talent war, you must build a culture where growth is visible, intentional, and undeniable. Here's the step-by-step playbook.

Step 1: Develop a Clearly Defined Path of Growth and Success for Your Employees

This is the foundation. Without it, every other effort is noise.

Your younger employees need more than vague and random promises of development. They need a structured, tangible roadmap that answers three questions:

- Where can I grow?
- Who will guide me?
- How will my growth create impact—for me and the company?

When employees can clearly see their future with you, they stay—and they become your most credible recruiters.

In WIN **#2** and WIN **#3,** we'll explore the two essential practices that make this path visible and sustainable.

Step 2: Audit Your Growth Path Visibility

Can a prospective hire spot a three-year growth trajectory within ten minutes of visiting your website or LinkedIn?

Do you have a careers page, and does it showcase real stories or generic HR jargon?

Do you have a job descriptions page, and does it highlight growth potential or just list duties?

Do you have social channels, and do they celebrate employee WINS or just high-level corporate outcomes?

If your growth culture isn't visible online, it doesn't exist in the talent market.

Step 3: Train Your Interview Teams

Your interviews are the tipping point. It's where your culture of growth is either brought to life—or exposed as empty words.

Every interviewer must be equipped to:

- Share their own growth journey
- Give examples of real internal advancement
- Speak confidently about mentorship and innovation opportunities

Candidates should walk away thinking:

"I'd feel safe in that environment—and I can see my future here."

If they don't, you're not attracting top talent. You're actively driving it away.

Step 4: Invest in Internal Case Studies

Real people. Real stories. Real growth.

Showcase employee journeys through videos, blogs, and social posts:

- From hire to leader
- From confusion to clarity
- From job to purpose

Key Insight: Highlight whole-life growth—not just promotions. Show how your culture helps people thrive personally and professionally.

When prospects see people like them winning, they'll believe they can too.

Step 5: Create a Reciprocal Growth Model

Growth is a two-way street.

In every interview, ask:

"How are you investing in your growth?"

"How do you want to grow?"

Then show them:

"Here's how we invest in growing our people."

This sets the tone: Growth isn't optional—it's expected.

Step 6: Empower Internal Advocates

Your most effective recruiters aren't HR. They're:

- The 26-year-old associate thriving in the Emerging Leaders structure
- The 30-year-old manager innovating new revenue streams
- The 23-year-old technician who found purpose through mentorship

When they post their stories, talent listens. Your culture becomes magnetic.

When they're silent? That's not disengagement—it's disappointment.

Fix it before they walk.

Actionable Insight: Launch a "Stories of Growth" Campaign

Every quarter, spotlight five employees who've experienced meaningful growth.

- Encourage them to share whole-life stories — not just career milestones. Share WINS!

- Let them narrate their journey in their own words.
- Share widely—careers page, social media, town halls.
- Celebrate it loudly.

Real stories attract real talent.

No growth stories? No talent pipeline. It's that simple.

BONUS: THE GENERATIONAL MAP OF MEANING

Generation | Primary Attraction Driver

- Baby Boomers: Stability & Retirement Benefits
- Gen X: Autonomy & Leadership Access
- Millennials: Purpose & Path of Growth
- Gen Z: Clarity, Coaching & Cultural Integrity

If you're using a **1990**s recruiting playbook for a **2025** workforce, you're already behind.

YOUR EMPLOYEE'S GROWTH STORY IS YOUR BRAND

Your culture is telling a story to the talent market every day.

The question is: Is it the story you want told?

Lead What's Next — Final Charge: WIN #1 – Attract the Talent Your Competitors Can't. Make Them Want In.

The days of posting a job and waiting for talent to come running are over. Top talent isn't looking for a job—they're looking for a journey. And if they can't see that journey with you, they won't even apply.

Attraction isn't about gimmicks or flashy marketing. It's about authenticity. It's about cultivating a workforce so visibly thriving that the outside world can't help but take notice. When your people flourish, they become your loudest recruiters and your strongest competitive edge.

Attraction isn't about gimmicks or flashy marketing. It's about authenticity.

Stop recruiting reactively. Start attracting intentionally. Because attraction gets them in the door, but engagement keeps them there—and that's where we're headed next.

BRIDGE TO WIN #2: GROWTH THAT ENGAGES

Attracting top talent is only step one.

The real challenge is keeping them growing.

In WIN **#2,** we'll unpack the tested practice that engages your younger workforce and elevates both productivity and loyalty.

But to activate the MAP in real time, your people need engagement they can feel. Chapter 6 unlocks an essential practice that turns connection into commitment.

CHAPTER 6

WIN #2 Engagement: Accountability Builds Trust. People Grow.

ONLY **4%** OF HR BUDGETS are allocated to employee engagement.

Meanwhile, **86%** of those same budgets are poured into recruiting—endlessly hunting for new talent, filling roles, and resetting the revolving door every **11–21** months.

This isn't just a misstep.

It's a leadership blind spot of historic proportions.

Because here's what my research and two decades of fieldwork unmistakably reveal:

Engagement isn't a side project – it's the engine. Employee engagement is the strongest predictor of whether you attract top talent, retain them, and unlock their highest level of performance.

It's the WIN that determines whether your organization thrives or unravels. Yet leaders spend more time managing performance than engineering engagement.

And the cost?

- Turnover bleeds institutional knowledge.
- Lost momentum paralyzes growth.

THE QUESTIONS THAT KEEP LEADERS UP AT NIGHT

Every week, I sit across from frustrated CEOs, HR executives, and team leaders who ask me the same questions:

> "*What does this younger workforce want from us?*"
>
> "*What do I have to do to keep them?*"

They're asking with an edge of exhaustion—as if they've tried everything:

- Hybrid schedules
- Wellness perks
- Mental health days
- Incentive bonuses

- Culture committees
- Unlimited PTO
- "Fun" initiatives masking deeper issues

And yet the exodus continues.

Because nothing is working.

Here's why:

The disconnect is profound—today's workforce is pursuing a fundamentally different kind of growth than older generations were taught to chase.

This chapter centers on one truth: engagement is not managed—it is built through accountability and trust. And the most effective structure for building both is small-group mentorship.

KEEP FLYING: THE ENGAGEMENT MOMENT THAT DETERMINES TRUST

When a high-potential employee tells you they're thinking about leaving, they're not resigning. They're testing whether engagement still has a future.

In that moment, there are only two outcomes. They jump—or they keep flying.

This is the moment leaders reveal whether trust has been built—or abandoned.

When Jim Hudson invited my friend Harry Gordon to fly in his open-cockpit plane, Harry expected a routine afternoon in the sky. The takeoff from Athens, Georgia was smooth. Calm air. Clear conditions. No warning signs.

Then, mid-flight over Winder, Georgia, Jim turned and asked, "Would you like to fly the plane?"

Harry had only flown twice before. But he took the controls.

And then Jim stood up—and jumped.

In an instant, Harry was alone at the stick. No preparation. No margin. Full responsibility.

Fear surged. His hands shook. The aircraft responded immediately. The plane didn't care about intention—only inputs. Stability wasn't emotional. It was structural.

Harry now had two options:

Panic and abandon the aircraft. Or stabilize, orient, and keep flying.

> *Clarity and trust eliminated hesitation; engagement followed.*

He locked onto visible landmarks. Recalled just enough training to regain control. Made small, corrective adjustments—one input at a time. Not the destination. Not the full flight. Just the next required move.

He kept flying.

Jim, meanwhile, jumped for a reason that had nothing to do with the aircraft—or the risk. There was a woman he wanted to impress in Winder. In his mind, the grass looked safer on the other side. He chose separation over structure. The landing was hard—injured, disappointed, and wrong about the certainty he expected. The aircraft he abandoned nearly paid the price for a decision driven by impulse instead of design.

Same uncertainty. Different structures. Predictable outcomes.

Your organization was not built for the runway or a hanger; it was built to fly. Employee engagement keeps it airborne.

When employees are seated in the cockpit—with a visible path, trusted relationships, and reinforced follow-through—they don't panic when pressure hits. They choose what the system has trained them to choose.

When clarity is missing, accountability is thin, and trust is assumed instead of engineered, people jump—for reasons that appear irrational only to leaders who never built the structure.

Harry kept flying—not because he felt ready, but because he was engaged in something larger than himself.

> *WIN **#2** is simple: when trust is engineered, engagement follows.*

THE LEADERSHIP RESPONSE THAT KEEPS PEOPLE FLYING

When a high-potential employee wavers, respond with a clear growth path (Clarity), defined expectations and ownership (Accountability), and relational reinforcement that says, "You don't fly alone" (Community).

THE 3 WINS OPERATING SYSTEM

Engagement does not happen because people feel motivated.

It happens because systems support accountability, trust, and belonging.

The **3** WINS Operating System is built on a timeless structural principle:

"*A cord of three strands is not quickly broken.*"

This is not poetry. It is physics.

ENGAGEMENT IS PRODUCED BY THREE INTERDEPENDENT STRANDS

Engagement becomes predictable—not fragile—when these three strands operate together:

- Clarity – a visible path people can trust
- Accountability – relationships that reinforce follow-through
- Community – belonging that turns effort into commitment

Remove one strand and the system weakens. Remove two and trust collapses. Remove all three—and engagement doesn't drift, it snaps.

The **3** WINS Operating System does not sit beside engagement. The three strands produce it.

HOW THE 3 WINS OPERATING SYSTEM IS USED

Clarity defines the path.

Accountability reinforces progress on the path.

Community sustains people while they walk it.

Clarity is installed through clearly documented maps of growth and success.

Accountability is reinforced through recurring relational touchpoints that make expectations visible and non-negotiable.

Trust and Community are sustained through small-group mentorship—where people are known, challenged, and supported as they grow.

When all three strands are active, engagement becomes predictable; and revenue follows as a direct outcome (WIN #**3**).

When one strand weakens, engagement erodes—not emotionally, but structurally.

STRAND ONE: CLARITY — THE PATH PEOPLE TRUST

Clarity answers the first question every engaged employee is asking:

Where is this going—and how do I grow here?

Clarity provides:

- A defined growth path
- Clear expectations
- Measurable progress
- A believable future

Without clarity, engagement never begins. Confusion breeds hesitation, and hesitation kills momentum.

But clarity alone is fragile.

Many organizations stop here—publishing career maps, role descriptions, and vision statements—then wonder why engagement still erodes. The reason is simple:

> *Clarity without reinforcement fades.*

STRAND TWO: ACCOUNTABILITY — THE RELATIONSHIPS THAT CREATE MOMENTUM

Accountability is not performance management. It is relational reinforcement.

Accountability answers the next question employees are silently asking:

"Who is walking this path with me—and will anyone notice if I drift?"

True accountability is created through:

- Consistent check-ins
- Shared ownership of growth
- Safe feedback loops

- Expectations held in relationship, not hierarchy

When accountability is missing, clarity becomes optional.

Goals blur. Standards slide. Follow-through weakens.

People disengage when expectations exist without connection.

Still, even clarity and accountability together are not enough.

People can know the path and be held to it—and still leave.

STRAND THREE: COMMUNITY — THE BELONGING THAT SUSTAINS COMMITMENT

Community answers the final question:

> *"Do I belong here—and does my growth matter to someone besides me?"*

Community transforms effort into commitment.

It creates:

- Psychological safety
- Shared struggle
- Mutual encouragement
- Identity beyond role

Community is what keeps people engaged when progress slows, when life gets heavy, or when growth becomes uncomfortable.

Without community, accountability becomes transactional and clarity becomes lonely.

Without community, people leave—even if everything else looks "right" on paper.

ENGAGEMENT IS NOT A FEELING — IT IS A SYSTEM

It must be designed.

The **3** WINS Operating System does not rely on charisma, perfect managers, or generational guesswork. It creates engagement by embedding trust, reinforcement, and belonging into the daily experience of work.

What structure consistently braids Clarity, Accountability, and Community into real life—not occasionally, but every week?

That structure is small-group mentorship. It doesn't treat symptoms—it removes the iguana.

THE GENERATIONAL DIVIDE: TWO MAPS OF SUCCESS

Older generations—Boomers and Gen X—were shaped by a work-first paradigm:

- Sacrifice now.
- Advance the career.
- Build security.
- Then, if there's time, build a life.

But Millennials and Gen Z see things differently.

They're not separating work from life; they're integrating the two. And they expect their jobs to contribute to who they're becoming, not just what they're earning.

According to my research project, **73%** of younger employees are seeking the following in the workplace:

- Whole-life growth: emotional maturity, financial confidence, relational strength, professional excellence.
- Whole-life success: work that fuels meaning, not just income.
- Whole-life connection: leaders and peers who see them as people, not just producers.

They're seeking growth that elevates the whole person—not just the employee.

It's alignment.

When the growth model shifts, engagement follows—or exits.

THEY'RE NOT DISENGAGED. THEY'RE DISILLUSIONED.

Younger employees aren't rejecting hard work.

They're resisting cultures where effort feels meaningless—where contribution lacks connection to purpose.

Disengagement rarely signals a performance issue—it almost always signals a growth issue.

Most leaders still treat engagement like a performance problem. It's not. It's a growth problem.

ISOLATION: THE SILENT SABOTEUR

Across the Emerging Leaders structures I actively lead—spanning multiple states, sectors, and company sizes—a striking pattern has become impossible to ignore. In every exit conversation with participants who fail to graduate, one theme surfaces with painful consistency: intentional isolation shrouded in individualism—not accidental, but chosen, defended, and even celebrated.

A CASE STUDY: WHEN STARBUCKS CHOSE UNITY

When Brian Niccol stepped into leadership at Starbucks in 2024, the company was plateauing. Stores were closing. Execution was inconsistent. The culture felt fragmented—less like one team and more like thousands of individual outposts.

His first move surprised people because it wasn't financial engineering or a flashy campaign. It was a unity move.

He reinstated a consistent dress standard across stores.

Not to control personalities. To protect cohesion. Unity is trust protection.

A team cannot trust what it cannot predict.

Niccol drew a clear line that created "we" again.

That's what strong leaders do in moments of drift: they don't negotiate cohesion. They restore it. And when cohesion returns, trust stabilizes—because people once again know what they're part of and what they're building together.

Leadership principle: When a culture fractures, your first job is not to motivate people —it's to reestablish the shared "we."

Unity isn't something leaders ask for. It's something they protect.

TRUST: THE HARD EDGE OF LEADERSHIP

Trust transforms individual talent into collective strength. When we honor the unique gifts of every human masterpiece—while refusing to let those gifts operate in isolation—a team stops being a cluster of capable people and becomes a unified force.

Where trust is absent, agendas dominate and silos calcify.

Where trust is present, people align, elevate one another, and accomplish what no individual ever could.

Trust is not a soft skill.

It is the hard edge of leadership—the platform that sets expectations, the foundation that sustains momentum, and the non-negotiable requirement for long-term growth. Trust is where cohesion is born and where individualism finally loses its power.

When leaders build trust with intention and protect it with courage, everything else—alignment, engagement, retention—finally has the strength to hold.

FROM THEORY TO PRACTICE: THE TRUST ENGINE

So, the real question becomes: How do we operationalize trust?

The most effective structure I've witnessed—the one that consistently turns trust into measurable outcomes—is the small-group mentorship practice.

Without a structure, trust erodes—and engagement collapses.

When leadership fails to align with their whole-life vision of success, younger employees don't revolt—they disengage. Some quietly check out. Others walk out.

If you don't fill that gap, your competitors will.

THE EMPHATIC PIVOT POINT: FROM PERKS TO PRACTICE

It's time to stop treating engagement as an HR initiative. Employee engagement is a core leadership responsibility.

You don't need flashier perks.

You don't need trendier tech, clever slogans, superficial culture campaigns.

What you need is a model that facilitates meaningful growth— personally, professionally, and relationally.

The solution isn't another program—it's a leadership practice.

WHAT YOUNGER EMPLOYEES REALLY WANT

Here's what Millennials and Gen Z consistently tell leaders they want:

- Growth that extends beyond titles, tasks, and training.
- Authentic conversations—not surface-level check-ins.
- Leaders who see them as people, not just performers.

Here's a strategic perspective that changes things:

A healthier employee outside your building is a more productive employee inside your building.

Whole-life investment creates whole-team performance.

The organization becomes the beneficiary of whole-life growth.

So how do you deliver that kind of growth?

THE MOST POWERFUL ENGAGEMENT TOOL: SMALL-GROUP MENTORSHIP

Across dozens of implementations, validated metrics reveal that the single most impactful lever for employee engagement is not:

- Bigger salaries
- Flexible schedules
- Free lunches

It's mentorship.

81% of Millennials and Gen Z say mentorship is critical to their success.

87% say they need success modeled—not merely described.

Yet only **21%** of BXer leaders report having any form of sustainable mentorship structure.

And in all my years working with hundreds of companies, I've found fewer than five had a truly effective, ongoing mentorship system.

If mentorship is this powerful, why do so few organizations get it right?

The problem isn't mentorship. The problem is outdated mentorship models that no longer resonate.

WHERE MOST MENTORSHIP FAILS

Every leadership team cycles through the same pattern with mentorship:

Create → Promote → Launch → Collapse

Within six months, the structure fades.

A year later, it disappears entirely.

A few years pass, the need resurfaces, and the cycle begins again — with the same outcome.

Leaders recognize the need—yet successful mentorship remains elusive.

CASE STUDY: WHEN GOOD INTENTIONS COLLAPSE

When the outcomes in my research project first pointed emphatically toward mentorship, I designed a structured model for a financial services client in Florida. They agreed, we launched, and I personally managed the rollout.

One year later, it was a monumental failure.

Perplexed, I interviewed and surveyed the seasoned leaders who served as mentors. Their feedback was consistent:

The **#1** reason why the traditional mentorship structure failed...

The mentors bailed.

Not out of apathy – but out of overwhelm.

"What do I read?"

"How do I prepare?"

"What do I even talk about?"

These weren't lazy leaders.

They were overwhelmed leaders.

Then I spoke with the younger employees—and the revelation became clear:

I had made the same mistake leaders have been making for thirty years.

Most companies still run mentorship like it's **1995**:

- Top-down, one-way conversations
- Stiff quarterly check-ins
- Executives "teaching" instead of collaborating
- Confined to a career focus

That model no longer resonates—and repeated evidence shows it fails to deliver sustainable results.

TODAY'S OPTIMIZED MENTORSHIP PRACTICE: WHAT ACTUALLY WORKS

- Small-group practice – where real growth occurs because people sharpen one another.
- Whole-life focused – extending beyond tasks to maturity, confidence, and long-term success.
- Collaborative – where the richest insights emerge not from a lecture, but from focused conversations where diverse perspectives collide.
- Experiential – grounded in real challenges, not theory.
- Relational – trust before titles; authenticity over authority.

THE NEW MENTORSHIP MODEL: WHOLE-LIFE. SCALABLE. TRANSFORMATIVE.

What It Looks Like

Whole-Life Focused:

This model develops emotional intelligence, relational strength, and leadership capacity.

This is the type of growth that stabilizes people—and scales organizations. This is the type of growth that fortifies trust.

Small-Group Based:

Groups of three to five employees, including the facilitator.

One hour per month.

- Small groups create accountability
- Accountability creates safety. Safety invites honesty.

This is where people elevate one another—where individual breakthroughs turn into a collective culture of trust and progress.

Cross-Departmental and Cross-Generational:

When employees connect across departments and generations:

- Communication strengthens
- Relationships deepen
- Trust expands across the entire organization

This type of growth must be intentionally designed and protected.

No Hierarchy:

Direct supervisors are never placed in groups with people who report to them.

Authenticity dies the moment evaluation enters the room.

If leaders want honest, transformative conversations, they must sit in rooms that reflect their level—not their authority.

Facilitator-Driven:

Choose facilitators for leadership potential—not tenure.

Small-group mentorship becomes a proving ground—a real-world leadership lab.

Many of the most effective facilitators are under **40** years old—because hunger to grow always outperforms years on the org chart.

Monthly Rhythm:

One hour.

Once a month.

It must be locked in and mandatory.

Consistency beats intensity—every time.

High-impact engagement isn't built in bursts—it's built in rhythm.

REAL RESULTS FROM REAL CONVERSATIONS

Every month, I write whole-life-focused mentorship lessons designed to spark transformation. Titles like:

"*Success Through Listening*"

"Success Through Teachability"

"Success Through Accountability"

"Success Through Decision-Making"

These aren't feel-good TED Talk topics.

They routinely:

- Save marriages
- Heal broken relationships
- Strengthen team trust
- Retain top talent
- Elevate emerging leaders

Every week, I hear from people whose lives are being quietly transformed—stories of struggle turning into strength.

Here are just a few excerpts:

> *"Four months ago, I felt like I was losing everything. The lesson on self-control helped me see where I was going wrong—and gave me the courage to make it right. Today, my marriage is healing, and I'm so thankful."* Ben, Florida

> *"I wasn't sure how I belonged in my small group. As the only Baby Boomer, I felt out of place at first. But over time, I learned how to connect with my kids and grandkids in*

ways I never thought possible. It's been life changing." Susan, Colorado

"The 'Success in the Valley' lesson opened a conversation where another group member and I realized we'd been carrying the same heavy burden for years—alone. Now, we're walking it out together." Perez, Charlotte

"A few months ago, I married my childhood sweetheart. And standing next to me that day as my best man, he wasn't a lifelong friend or a family member. It was a guy from my small group at work. Your impact runs deeper than you realize." Aaron, Georgia

Who is the benefactor of this type of transformation?

You. Your culture. Your bottom line!

When employees grow outside of work, they bring their whole selves back to work. This isn't a theory; it's a fact—the numbers are loud.

THE METRICS DON'T LIE

Here are a few metrics from my clients that have implemented the small-group, whole-life focused mentorship practice:

63%

---

higher retention in mentored departments

- **62%** increase in team trust scores
- **32%** increase in cross-functional collaboration
- **41%** more employee-led revenue initiatives

There are other outcomes I've seen consistently emerge from the small-groups:

- Stronger accountability
- Healthier internal relationships
- Better cross-department communication
- A fortified sense of community
- Elevated productivity
- Durable trust

And here's the leadership paradox:

Employees in mentorship groups are more productive—despite spending one fewer hour per month on task work.

It's not a loss.

It's an investment that produces dividends.

BEYOND GROWTH: MENTAL HEALTH AND CULTURAL GLUE

In a world where burnout and anxiety are at an all-time high, these groups become more than leadership development—they've become a lifeline.

Employees use them to:

- Process pressure in a healthy way
- Support each other through personal and professional challenges
- Build trust that transcends roles, departments, and hierarchies

Several years ago, I spoke to an executive team of a large financial services company. We met in a penthouse conference room above the Atlanta skyline. As I explained the small-group model, I noticed the CEO's eyes well with tears.

I gently asked:

"*Are you okay?*"

He paused and said, "Last year, my son took his own life. He worked for this company—the company I run. In his final letter, he wrote, 'I don't have anyone to talk to about my struggle.' I just realized... if we had something like this in place—

this small-group practice—my son might still be here today."

I'm not claiming that small-group mentorship is the solution to the mental health crisis.

It creates a safe space for people to be seen, heard, and supported—sometimes that changes everything.

These groups embody the very heart of the phrase, "Iron sharpens iron." We strengthen one another— not by fixing each other's problems, but by choosing to walk together through them.

Here's the reality—when we create this kind of environment, everyone benefits. The people. The culture. The bottom line.

Healthy people build healthy organizations. And the ripple effect touches every corner—culturally, financially, and long-term growth.

LET'S TALK ABOUT TRUST

Trust isn't just a nice-to-have. It's the glue holding your culture together.

Trust is the foundation of performance. Without it, execution breaks down.

My research uncovered two alarming truths:

- **61%** of Millennials and Gen Z say, "I do not trust my employer to ensure my growth."
- **68%** say, "I do not trust my co-worker to make decisions in my best interest."

A trust pandemic is quietly eroding organizational structures. And if trust isn't built intentionally, it becomes a silent leak—slow at first, then it fuels collapse.

So, how do we intentionally build trust?

Here's the formula:

> *Vulnerability + Transparency = Trust*

Where does this happen consistently?

Inside every mentorship group.

This is the beauty of the practice—it creates a safe space for vulnerability and transparency to flourish. As trust grows, so does your organization's strength.

Thriving trust isn't just cultural. It's life giving. It's the engine of sustainable growth.

THE SECRET TO TRUE ENGAGEMENT: RECIPROCAL ACCOUNTABILITY

Yes—I'm back to accountability. And for good reason.

Accountability isn't one gate among many. It is the gate through which every leader must pass to achieve sustainable growth. But here's the catch: accountability can't be passive. It must be active and reciprocal.

For decades, leaders have held employees accountable for performance. That's nothing new. But today, as we have discussed, the paradigm has shifted. Now, employees are holding leaders accountable— not just for workplace results, but for creating an environment where they can experience whole-life growth and success.

If you refuse to—or simply fail to—build this structure, your people may remain physically present—but mentally and emotionally, they are already gone.

To produce the results promised by your clearly defined path of growth and success, the path must include the life-giving practice of small-group mentorship.

It's not optional. It's not "nice-to-have."

It's an essential, non-negotiable component—because it's where trust is built, growth is fostered, and engagement is reignited.

This is the line in the sand.

As a leader, you're not just responsible for this—you're being held accountable to facilitate this life-giving practice. Your people are already measuring your leadership by it—your future employees and your bottom line will be impacted by this decision to either facilitate small-group mentorship practice or not.

To WIN employee engagement:

It isn't just about telling people what to do.

It's about helping them build who they become.

THE OVERLOOKED VARIABLE IN MERGERS & ACQUISITION: SUCCESSFULLY IMPLEMENTING A CULTURE BRIDGE

In merger and acquisition mode, leaders focus on:

- Products
- Services
- Assets
- Clients
- A/R and A/P

But they often miss the most volatile variable:

The culture they're inheriting.

Think about it—your organization is in acquisition mode because you've done the hard work of building a strong, healthy culture. That's your edge. Your competitive advantage.

But the company you're acquiring is bringing a struggling culture—one that doesn't align with yours. This isn't just a mismatch. It's a collision waiting to happen.

What happens when two cultures collide without intervention?

Chaos. Attrition. Division. Loss of Revenue.

Sometimes—even complete collapse.

And nowhere is engagement—and the trust that fuels it—more tested than during an acquisition.

CULTURE BRIDGES: WHAT HAPPENS WHEN YOU DON'T BUILD THEM

The CEO of Trueline Infrastructure Solutions called me one afternoon with a voice that carried both pride and concern. His company had acquired four smaller firms within twelve months, positioning Trueline to become one of the nation's top cell-tower builders. On paper, everything looked perfect—stronger market presence, expanded capacity, and a wider competitive moat.

But inside the company, something was quietly breaking.

Those acquisitions didn't just bring new assets —they brought four entirely different cultures. When those cultures collided, what looked like growth on a spreadsheet turned into chaos in real time.

The CEO admitted that in their race to close the deals, the private equity firm overlooked the one variable they couldn't afford to miss—the culture they were inheriting (purchasing).

They didn't just acquire companies. They acquired four cultural time bombs.

In response, they invited me to speak to the combined leadership teams. But as each group shared their perspective, one theme echoed again and again:

"*We do not trust them.*"

The trust crisis wasn't subtle—it was systemic.

We prepared to launch a small-group mentorship practice to bridge the cultures.

But we never got the chance.

The internal fractures quickly widened. Within two weeks of filing for bankruptcy, the company shut its doors—and hundreds of people lost their jobs.

The lesson? A company can buy assets, customers, and capacity. But without a proven method to build trust across every acquisition, the culture it inherits will collapse the strategy meant to secure its future.

Then there's the other path—the one most leaders never realize is possible.

THE POWER OF BUILDING THE BRIDGE BEFORE YOU CROSS IT

Not long after the Trueline collapse, I received a very different kind of phone call from Phil Kelley, CEO of Salem One. His voice didn't carry fear or urgency—it carried foresight.

> "Kent," *he said,* "*we're in high-growth mode. Acquisitions are positioning us to expand into the fastest-growing zone in the United States. But with that growth comes two potential threats that could derail everything.*"
>
> He paused.

"First, if we grow faster than we develop our people, we'll create a leadership deficit. Second, we must protect our culture. Salem One is healthy, strong, and thriving—we cannot afford to lose that. And we want every employee in the acquired companies to join that culture, not fracture it."

This was a CEO who understood the truth too many leaders ignore: Growth is not the problem. Unprepared people—and unintegrated cultures—are.

So together, we built something powerful.

We designed an Emerging Leaders structure composed of young leaders across all three Salem One locations. Inside that structure, we launched a small-group mentorship practice with one intentional aim:

Embed trust. Build relationships. Create cross-campus alignment before the culture had the chance to drift.

And it continues to bear fruit.

We built culture bridges into the newly acquired companies on a foundation of trust—so employees weren't just assimilating; they were connecting. Not superficially. Not organizationally. But relationally.

The results were undeniable:

- Strong, healthy relationships across all campuses
- Cross-campus communication happening daily
- Cross-campus revenue generation—driven by leaders who now knew and trusted one another
- Emerging leaders forming authentic relationships with people they would not know without intentional design.

While other companies crumble under the weight of acquisition growth, Salem One continues to be fortified—strengthened by a culture built on trust, accountability, deliberate development of its people, and a deep bench of future leaders.

The contrast could not be clearer: One company collapsed because trust was ignored. Another is thriving because trust was engineered.

Salem One didn't gamble on culture. They built it. And growth followed.

BUILD THE BRIDGE BEFORE THE BREAK HAPPENS:

So, beyond the balance sheets, what's the solution to fortifying a successful acquisition?

A culture bridge—built through trust.

The fastest, most effective way to build a cultural bridge between organizations is to launch small-group mentorship—leveraging your people from the healthy culture as anchors.

The results?

- Instantly open communication channels
- Accelerated relationship building
- And most importantly—elevated trust across both organizations

This cannot be left to chance. If a culture of trust isn't intentionally implemented, it will default to the lowest common denominator—and your acquisition ROI will pay the price.

The bridge you build today determines whether your cultures merge or fracture tomorrow. Start with your people. Start with small-group mentorship. It's how you transform uncertainty and skepticism into committed contributors united under one thriving culture.

LEADERSHIP REFLECTION: ARE YOU WORTH FOLLOWING?

Ask yourself:

- Do your employees have a safe place to process beyond tasks?

- Are future leaders shaped intentionally—or accidentally?
- Is mentorship a checkbox—or a culture builder?

The absence of this structure doesn't reveal uncertainty. It reveals delay. This is your opportunity.

Lead What's Next — Final Charge: Ignite the Revival.

Engagement isn't about perks. It's about people. It's the system leaders build that determines whether people stay engaged—or step away.

When trust is engineered, engagement becomes predictable.

When engagement becomes predictable, retention follows. Trust determines whether a culture compounds—or collapses.

The next WIN explains why retention isn't an HR initiative. It's your most profitable growth strategy.

RECAP: THE WIN #2 PLAYBOOK: HOW TO BUILD SMALL-GROUP MENTORSHIP THAT ACTUALLY WORKS

- Define the goal: engagement through trust + whole-life growth.
- Select cross-generational, cross-departmental groups of three to five people. Place supervisors and executives in their own groups.
- Choose facilitators for hunger and potential, not tenure.
- Establish the monthly rhythm: one-hour, same time, every month.
- Provide whole-life lesson content (like "Success Through Listening," etc.).
- Measure impact: retention, trust scores, collaboration, and employee-led revenue.

And when engagement becomes part of your culture, retention becomes predictable. Chapter 7 reveals why retention isn't an HR program—it's your most profitable revenue strategy.

A map may attract someone to the path—but only what happens next determines whether they stay on it.

CHAPTER 7

WIN #3:

Retention

Community Turns Retention into Revenue.

WIN **#3** is simple: when the future is clear and shared, people stay—and revenue follows. When it isn't, they leave.

EMPLOYEE TENURE HAS COLLAPSED at an unprecedented rate.

SIXTEEN MONTHS: THE HIDDEN EXPIRATION DATE

- Baby Boomers: **19.1** years
- Gen X: **10.2** years
- Millennials: **21** months
- Gen Z: **11** months

Your largest workforce segment—Millennials and Gen Z—averages just sixteen months of tenure.

Not sixteen years. Not sixteen quarters. Sixteen months.

Given that reality, your choice is stark: keep bleeding cash or start building revenue. You can either keep viewing employee retention as an expense—or utilize it as a revenue engine. Because once you make the shift, retention stops draining your margins and starts fueling them.

That's the choice. One drains you. One scales you. Only one builds your future.

To help you make that shift, ask yourself:

- Can you hit any meaningful growth targets with a workforce turning over every **1.5** years?
- Can you protect culture, brand strength, and institutional knowledge when your best people leave just as they're gaining momentum?
- Can you maintain operational fluidity when your leadership pipeline evaporates every **16** months?
- Can you truly outperform competitors when you're constantly retraining instead of advancing?

The answer is obvious: No.

And if high-potential talent keeps turning over every year, you're not facing a hiring problem.

You're facing an architecture problem. A structural flaw. A design gap. A clarity void.

The younger workforce is the challenge leaders fear—and the emerging workforce is the opportunity they're overlooking.

And it is quietly draining:

- Your culture
- Your operations
- Your margins
- Your credibility

This is the turning point:

Redesign your structure, and retention becomes untouchable—an advantage no competitor can replicate or steal.

This is how organizations stabilize. This is how cultures strengthen. This is how revenue grows.

Not by accident. Not by perks. But by design.

THE REAL COST OF LOSING THEM

It's not just painful when your people walk out the door, it's expensive.

$34,000

The average cost of losing just one Millennial or Gen Z employee.

That's not a guess. That's not a theory. That number is real data, real exits, and real losses—reinforced by executive teams across nearly every industry I work with.

And here's the alarming part:

I've reviewed the P&L statements of hundreds of companies—from fast-growing startups to Fortune 500s—and I almost never see that cost accurately accounted for in the financial accounts.

Why? Because it hides in plain sight.

It doesn't show up as a single line item. It trickles out—quietly bleeding profit while the business hums forward, unaware. Until the culture weakens. Until the margins tighten. Until the talent well runs dry.

In nearly every leadership session I facilitate, I ask a simple question:

> "*How much does it cost your organization to replace one employee?*"

And every time—without fail—leaders come back and say:

> "*Your* **$34,000** *estimate is too low.*"

The consensus? It costs at least one full year's salary for every person who walks out your door.

Now—do the math on your retention losses.

Think about your last ten exits. Now multiply that by their annual salaries. Then add the cost of downtime, lost momentum, and stalled projects. Now ask yourself—can we really afford this?

Still not convinced? Here's a small sample of what leaders tell me every single week:

- A CEO of a large CPA firm in Atlanta told me that they lose on average **30** CPAs per quarter. **$34,000** (expense per lost employee) X **30** employees = **$1,020,000**
- A healthcare CEO hires **90** employees per year in hopes that she'll retain **20**. **$34,000** X **70** = **$2,380,000**

- An HVAC founder hired **74** employees in **12** months... and lost **72**. **$34,000** X **72** = **$2,448,000**
- A New England print company hired **16** employees... and lost **7**—almost half. **$34,000** X **7** = **$238,000**

These aren't outliers. These are daily realities —inside high-pressure environments led by well-meaning, capable people.

They're not failing because they don't care. They're failing because they don't see the drain. They've accepted turnover as a cost of doing business.

Over time, the pace of turnover becomes familiar—even expected—and leaders adjust without realizing the long-term cost.

And it's killing their ability to grow.

CONCEPT → REVENUE IS NOT...

- classroom exercise
- brainstorming for fun
- leadership simulation
- hypothetical innovation

CONCEPT → REVENUE IS...

- A structured process to identify real growth opportunities for your company.

During one of my Vistage talks in the Midwest, a frustrated CEO blurted out, "Kent... I'm doing everything I can to run a business, but every day I realize I'm actually operating a revolving door."

The real cost isn't just financial—it's cultural, operational, and deeply emotional: lost productivity, broken momentum, declining morale, fragmented culture, and the erosion of institutional knowledge.

These aren't numbers in a spreadsheet. They're cracks in the foundation of your future.

And they don't stop until you do. Until you say:

"No *more.*"

No more passive acceptance. No more reactive hiring.

It's time to lead with intentionality.

Build what retains. Invest in what remains. Start constructing a workforce that will scale your vision, not drain it.

Talent loss isn't primarily a staffing issue. It's a leadership decision—and one that becomes far easier to solve with the right structure. And the cost of waiting is already on your books.

THE POSITIVE PIVOT: WHY THIS IS ACTUALLY GOOD NEWS

Here's the upside: you can fix this—and if you do, it becomes your competitive edge.

Because most of your competitors won't.

They'll keep burning cash on churn. They'll keep absorbing turnover as a cost of doing business. They'll keep believing "young people just don't want to work," and that belief will keep draining their margins.

But you're reading this because you lead differently.

You're ready to replace assumptions with architecture. You're ready to stop gambling on retention and start engineering retention with intention.

Retention isn't about holding people in place. It's about giving them a reason to stay.

When you deliver that reason with clarity, structure, and intention, everything changes. Culture strengthens, loyalty rises, productivity accelerates, and your company becomes the place top performers seek for long-term growth.

This is the moment leadership stops reacting and starts designing.

So yes—the generational departure curve is real. But so is your ability to rise above retention.

That's leadership. That's the shift. And it starts now.

To make this shift with confidence, two non-negotiable practices must anchor the path forward. We've examined the first—Small-Group Mentorship. Now it's time to unpack the second.

- Small-Group Mentorship - where development is personal, feedback is consistent, and progress is visible.
- Respected Voice - where contribution is recognized, valued, and tied to real impact.

When these two practices are present, retention stops functioning as a cost center and begins operating as a revenue engine—an advantage no competitor can buy, copy, or duplicate.

And here's what makes these practices so necessary:

These employees didn't join your company to leave your company.

They applied because they saw potential. They accepted because they trusted your mission. They arrived believing they could build a future inside your walls—not somewhere else.

When that future never materializes, they don't complain.

They disconnect. They detach. They drift away long before they resign.

First emotionally. Then mentally.

By the time they resign, they've been gone for months.

They don't leave because of perks or pay. They leave because they don't see progress—personal progress.

You hold them accountable for performance. They hold you accountable for direction.

That's not entitlement. That's maturity—and it's redefining loyalty across every industry.

And at the epicenter of that new definition of loyalty is voice.

THE VOICE FACTOR: WHAT MATTERS MORE THAN PAY AND PROMOTIONS

The **#1** reason why your younger workforce stays?

It's not the paycheck, although pay matters. It's not the perks. It's not even the promotion.

It's voice—respected voice.

My research shows this loud and clear:

The top reason Millennials and Gen Z remain with their employer is because they feel heard.

Not just acknowledged. Not just praised.

Heard. As in: "I have a voice here that matters."

That voice is the gateway to ownership—and ownership is the foundation of loyalty.

A GENERATIONAL SHIFT IN LOYALTY DRIVERS

Older generations were trained to chase titles and salary bumps. That was the currency of commitment.

But your younger employees? They're operating from a different set of loyalty drivers.

They want to contribute. They want to influence. They want to build something that reflects their ideas.

And here's where many seasoned leaders panic:

"You're telling me Sarah—who's only been here six months—wants a respected voice?

Or she'll leave?"

Yes. That's exactly what I'm saying. But don't misunderstand the point.

It's not entitlement. It's investment.

What younger employees are really saying is:

"I believe in your mission. I align with your values. I want to grow my career here. But you're struggling to connect with my generation—both as employees and as customers. I can help. Just give me a voice."

And the data shows exactly how much that voice matters.

WHAT THE DATA REVEALS ABOUT LOYALTY

Here's what the numbers show with startling clarity:

When asked whether the opportunity to formally present growth ideas influence their decision to stay at a company—

- **73%** of Zillennials said YES.
- Just **27%** of BXers said YES.

Why such a large difference? It isn't a criticism of BXers. They entered a workplace built on a straightforward exchange: do the work, earn the paycheck, stay the course. And they delivered.

But they were never invited into a culture where growth ideas were expected, requested, or rewarded. The paycheck was the structure—and for decades, it was enough.

For today's emerging workforce, it isn't—the paycheck is merely the starting line.

Their real motivator? Having a meaningful voice—being an active participant in shaping the future of your company.

This single shift in what defines loyalty changes everything about how leaders must engage, develop, and retain their teams.

VOICE ISN'T A PERK—IT'S A GROWTH STRATEGY

Let's reframe this:

Voice isn't a threat to your leadership. It's fuel for your growth.

When you activate voice, you don't lose control—you gain momentum. You create a culture where ideas are owned, innovation is shared, and loyalty runs deep.

That's not softness. That's strategy. And it works.

Give them a voice—and you'll keep their talent, their energy, and their loyalty.

That's the WIN-WIN.

STOP BURNING MONEY: THE HIDDEN COST OF EMPTY CULTURE SPEND

There's one truth I can guarantee about your workforce—without even knowing them:

Not one employee has ever said:

"I was about to accept a better job offer, but then I remembered that amazing July 4th cookout. I just can't leave now."

Let's be real:

- The Christmas party
- The company picnic
- Taco Tuesdays and swag bags

They don't retain employees. They might boost morale for a day—but when it comes to reducing turnover and building long-term loyalty, the ROI is abysmal.

And I've seen it firsthand. After analyzing dozens of P&L statements across industries, one pattern jumps off the page:

Companies are spending hundreds of thousands on "culture events" with zero retention return.

Yes—community matters. Team bonding has value. But let's be honest:

None of it moves the revenue needle or the **3** WINS that actually matter in the war for talent.

REFRAME ROI: RETENTION ON INVESTMENT

Ask yourself:

- Are your "culture spends" retaining talent?
- Is there a measurable drop in turnover?
- Are your people staying because they feel deeply connected to your business?

You already know the answer.

People don't stay for parties. They stay for purpose.

They stay when they believe they matter—when their voice is heard, and their ideas have impact.

WHAT THE DATA ACTUALLY SAYS

My research doesn't show "holiday parties" or "free snacks" as the top reason Millennial or Gen Z employees stay.

Not even close.

They stay when their voice carries weight. They stay when their future is visible. They stay when they're trusted to help build what comes next.

So, the real question is:

What's the practical solution that activates voice, retains talent, drives revenue, is easy to implement, and reduces wasteful expenditure?

If clarity is the staying power and voice is the loyalty engine, then you need a repeatable system that operationalizes both—not once, but every year.

CONCEPT TO REVENUE: THE RETENTION FRAMEWORK THAT WORKS

This is more than a feel-good initiative. This is not a theory.

A core practice of WIN **#3** is Concept to Revenue—an annual activation event that converts respected voice into measurable revenue and long-term retention. Concept to Revenue isn't just an innovation engine; it's a retention engine delivered through an innovation event.

It's a tested, revenue-generating system I've deployed across manufacturing, engineering/architecture, financial services, logistics, and nonprofit leadership.

Voice identifies your future leaders. Concept to Revenue develops them.

CONCEPT TO REVENUE (ANNUAL EVENT)

A practical four-month framework designed to:

- Activate employee ideation voice
- Fuel frontline innovation and problem solving
- Build cross-departmental trust
- Surface future leaders
- Generate real, measurable revenue

HOW IT WORKS: A 4-MONTH INNOVATION ENGINE

Step 1 — Cast the Vision: Form Innovation Groups

Bring the organization together to introduce the Concept-to-Revenue initiative and align everyone around the purpose and path forward.

- Use your existing small-groups from the mentorship structure.
- Assign three to five employees per group.
- Cross departments, tenures, roles, and generations.

- Establish clear ground rules: respect, contribution, collaboration.
- Commit to **1.5** hours per month – any additional work happens "off the clock."
- Determine the rewards for winning.

This step sets the cultural tone: innovation is not an executive privilege; it's a shared responsibility.

Step 2 – Month 1: Ideation

Each group identifies one business opportunity, pain point, or revenue idea.

Every Idea Must Pass Three Tests:

- Is the opportunity or problem real? Do customers or employees actually experience it—or clearly want it?
- Would someone pay for the solution? Does it create real value?
- Can we execute it? Does it align with our capabilities and strategy?

Real innovation doesn't begin in a retreat center or an executive suite – it begins here, with the people who experience your business every day. Cross-department and cross-generation dialogue produces a surge of ownership and engagement that no incentive program can replicate.

Step 3 – Month 2: Implementation Planning

Teams shift from ideation to building. They begin thinking like owners—not employees.

They create:

- A tactical roadmap
- KPIs and success metrics
- A resource outline and projected ROI

This is where momentum accelerates. The competition becomes real. Energy rises. Ideas sharpen. Groups begin to see themselves not as participants, but as contributors to the future of the business.

Step 4 – Month 3: Presentation Coaching

Each group receives targeted development:

Groups receive presentation training with real-time feedback, with a clear understanding that every team member must have an active role during the pitch—no passengers. Everyone owns the outcome.

And here's the differentiator: I remove technology from the process—no slides, no screens. Why? Because it forces clarity. Leaders evaluate the idea, not the polish.

Each team receives a tri-fold science project board. If a concept can't be explained clearly enough to fit on that board, it isn't ready for execution.

This step builds confidence, communication skill, and leadership presence—regardless of tenure or title.

Step 5 — Month 4: The Main Event: Concept to Revenue Day

This is an event—high energy, high stakes, high engagement.

Each group steps onto a stage and presents to executive leadership in a "Shark Tank" format:

- 5 minutes to pitch
- 5 minutes of Q&A

Winning ideas receive:

- Resources
- Executive support
- Public recognition
- Fast-tracked implementation

This structure shatters silos, strengthens trust, and creates cross-organizational buy-in. It builds the kind of cultural momentum parties and picnics can only pretend to create.

Instead of pouring money into one-off morale events, invest in an annual ideation competition that solves retention, boosts engagement, sparks ownership, and generates revenue. It's a no-brainer.

One employee at an architecture firm told me:

> "*The moment leadership took my growth idea seriously was the moment I decided to build my career here.*"

At every client where Concept to Revenue is active, I can walk into the building today and someone will pull me aside—often in sworn secrecy—to share the idea they're preparing for next year. That's the power of voice turned into ownership.

CASE STUDY: $13.1 MILLION IN NEW VALUE

Theory is irrelevant unless it produces results. And results are exactly what Concept to Revenue delivers.

Concept to Revenue isn't a program—it's a cultural pillar. For five consecutive years, one of my clients has used it to unlock innovation, drive growth, and transform their workforce from the inside out.

In year one, the rewards were modest: the winning team received **$200** Amazon gift cards.

By year four, the stakes—and the outcomes—had skyrocketed.

$13.1M

A single winning idea generated **$13.1 million** in new revenue in year four.

And by year five, they took recognition to a new level, rewarding winning teams with luxury vacations and high-end prizes.

Why such dramatic escalation? Because when employees see their ideas shape the company's future, everything changes. They step into ownership. They think bigger. They act bolder.

Some teams developed ideas so strong and so profitable that the company created entirely new roles for them—positions these employees effectively carved out for themselves, managing revenue streams worth millions annually. They weren't waiting for promotions that didn't exist. They built their own.

But the deeper ROI runs far beyond dollars:

- Belief in leadership

- Belief in their own potential
- Belief that they belong

The most common statements we hear at these events?

> *"My growth ideas were respected and heard."*
>
> *"I used to see my job as a task list. Now I see it as a launching pad."*

This is what happens when leaders stop demanding buy-in and start giving their people a voice.

WHY CONCEPT TO REVENUE WORKS

- Gives employees voice and ownership
- Drives retention through meaning, not perks
- Builds business literacy and growth mindsets
- Reveals hidden talent and future leaders
- Creates healthy internal competition
- Breaks down silos and drives collaboration
- Directly connects people to purpose and revenue

LEADERSHIP REFLECTION: HOW DO YOU SHOW THE FUTURE?

Ask yourself:

- Can every team member articulate their next growth opportunity?
- Have you created a structure where employee ideas are heard and valued?
- Do you treat internal innovation like your next best investment?

If not, you're running a culture of confusion—not retention. You're running a culture of stagnation—with a burnout cycle hiding behind free snacks.

STOP SPENDING ON PERKS. START INVESTING IN PURPOSE.

Unlimited PTO doesn't build purpose.

Corn hole competitions do not build trust.

Free lunches don't build legacy.

Your competitors keep entertaining employees, convinced that fun equals retention. Entertainment doesn't build loyalty.

They stay because they matter.

Want to keep your best people? Give them a stage, not a script. Give them a problem, not a pizza. Give them purpose.

And when you build purpose, clarity, and voice into your culture... you'll attract top talent with the **3** WINS!

NITRO FUEL FOR GROWTH

Most organizations are pouring money into perks that feel good but change nothing. Free lunches don't create loyalty. Events don't build trust. And culture campaigns don't replace structure.

What actually works is investing in systems that give people voice, direction, and ownership. When employees see a future inside your organization, they stop looking for one elsewhere. That's not motivation—that's design.

BEYOND THE PROGRAM: MAKE RETENTION PART OF YOUR CULTURE

This isn't about launching a shiny initiative and calling it innovation. It's about embedding retention and innovation into the soul of your culture.

How?

- Normalize Intentional Growth Opportunities: Make growth through ideation a fixed practice.

- Celebrate Internal Innovation: Treat in-house ideas like gold. Spotlight them. Fund them. Scale them.
- Reward Risk and Effort: Don't just reward perfect results—reward bold effort. Celebrate resilience and problem-solving.

The Concept to Revenue practice satisfies these criteria—while increasing revenue.

Lead What's Next — Final Charge: WIN #3: Retention is a Strategic Advantage. Retention is Revenue.

Retention isn't about handcuffs. It's about anchors. Anchors of:

- Purpose
- Clarity
- Contribution
- Community
- Ownership

That's how you WIN the war for talent. That's how you build a culture that lasts.

Final Charge: Anchor the Future

Your younger workforce doesn't want to be retained. They want to be respected. They want to grow. They want to matter.

When people see a future inside your organization, they help build it. When they don't, they quietly prepare to leave.

Retention isn't a program. It's a structure.

And when that structure is built intentionally —through clarity, trust, and voice— people don't just stay. They invest.

Retention is not the result of effort. It is the outcome of design.

CHAPTER 8

The Growth System That WINS — And the Leaders Who Install It

> *Clarity attracts. Accountability engages. Community retains.*

EVERYTHING IN THIS BOOK has been building toward one outcome:

Ownership.

You've seen the data. You've felt the tension. You understand the cost of getting this wrong—and the opportunity waiting if you get it right.

At this point, there is no ambiguity left.

The younger workforce is not the problem. The absence of structure is.

And now—you know the structure.

THIS IS NOT A PHILOSOPHY

Most leadership books ask you to think differently.

This one requires you to build differently.

The **3** WINS Operating System is not a concept to admire. It is a system to install.

Because growth is not an outcome of intention. It is the result of architecture.

And architecture either produces:

- alignment
- engagement
- retention
- revenue

—or it produces:

- confusion
- friction
- attrition
- loss

There is no neutral system.

You already have one.

The only question is:

Is it producing what you want?

THE THREE OUTCOMES ARE NOT OPTIONAL

Every organization is producing three outcomes right now—intentionally or accidentally:

- You are attracting talent... or repelling it
- You are engaging your people... or disengaging them
- You are retaining momentum... or restarting it

The difference is not effort.

It is structure.

The **3** WINS Operating System aligns that structure to produce:

Clarity → Accountability → Community

And when those three strands operate together:

You don't hope for growth. You engineer it.

THIS IS THE POINT OF NO RETURN

From this moment forward, you cannot claim confusion about your workforce.

You cannot blame:

- a generation
- a market
- or a mindset

You now understand the system required to lead them.

Which means the variable is no longer knowledge.

The variable is decision.

YOU HAVE TWO PATHS

You can return to:

- reacting
- adjusting
- explaining
- hoping

Or you can install:

- clarity that defines the path
- accountability that reinforces growth

- community that secures commitment

One path sustains pressure.

The other produces momentum.

WHAT WINNING ACTUALLY LOOKS LIKE

Winning is not:

- better perks
- louder mission statements
- or faster hiring cycles

Winning looks like this:

- Your best people stay—and grow.
- Your culture stabilizes—and strengthens.
- Your organization attracts talent without chasing it.
- Your leaders lead with confidence—not concern.

You're not building a workforce. You're building people.

Your people become business builders.

And your revenue reflects it.

Not occasionally.

Predictably.

INSTALL THE SYSTEM

If you want to WIN:

- Build the map. Make growth visible.
- Open the gate. Make accountability active.
- Strengthen the bond. Build community that people commit to.
- Do it consistently. Do it structurally. Do it without compromise.

And the outcomes will follow.

Not by chance.

By design.

THE LEADERS WHO WILL WIN NEXT

The next generation of great organizations will not be defined by:

- brand
- scale
- or history

They will be defined by:

- their ability to attract, engage, and retain the people who drive growth

And that ability will not come from inspiration.

It will come from installation.

The organizations that will define the next decade will not be the ones with the best strategy on paper. They will be the ones with the strongest system in practice.

Because strategy can inspire— but only structure sustains.

And in a workforce that no longer waits, guesses, or settles— the leaders who win will be the ones who build environments where growth is visible, accountability is trusted, and community is real.

Not occasionally. Systematically.

THE FINAL DECISION

The younger workforce is already moving.

They are choosing:

- where to build
- where to grow
- and where to stay

The only question left is:

> *Will they choose you?*

Because if you do not define their path, they will define it without you.

And if they cannot see a future with you, they will build one somewhere else.

Final Charge

This is how organizations WIN.

Not occasionally. Not accidentally. Systematically.

> *Clarity attracts. Accountability engages. Community retains.*

You don't need another strategy. You need the system.

Now install it.

3 WINS!

A brief About the Author / How to work with Dr. Wessinger

www.ingramcontent.com/pod-product-compliance
Lightning Source LLC
LaVergne TN
LVHW091149080826
845145LV00008B/2306

9781969826122